Should My Past Be Honored?
My Perilous Journey Out of Nigeria

Should My Past Be Honored? My Perilous Journey Out of Nigeria

Jerry H. Anyaene

Copyright © 2023 Jerry H. Anyaene

All rights reserved. This book or any portion thereof may not be reproduced or used in any manner whatsoever without the express written permission of the publisher except for the use of brief quotations in a book review.

ISBN: 978-0-578-96089-0

Dedication

I dedicate this book to my children:
Chijioke Odili Chukwu, Ifeanyi Chukwu, and my stepdaughter Marjorie.

Foreword

When I first heard Brother Jerry Anyaene's heartwarming testimony about his life, the scripture that came to mind was Proverbs 19:21, NKJV: "There are many plans in a man's heart. Nevertheless the Lord's counsel—that will stand."

Life is a journey of uncertainties, but faith is the seed of greatness and success, no matter the challenges or difficulties life presents. After salvation, the greatest discovery is to find your purpose in life and fulfill it. To achieve this is to totally submit your own will and desires to those of God.

This road can be daunting with many challenges, but it is made easier when you obey God's word in Proverbs 3:5–6, NKJV: "Trust in the Lord with all your heart and lean not on your own understanding; in all your ways acknowledge Him, and He shall direct your paths."

The Lord will eventually direct your paths. That was what the Master did for Jerry.

I recommend this book to anyone or any group of people struggling to find purpose and fulfill their divine destinies. The story of Jerry Anyaene will inspire you greatly.

Sam Korankye Ankrah
Apostle General,
Royalhouse Chapel International

Contents

Foreword · vii

Chapter 1	An Unusual Childhood · · · · · · · · · · · · · · · · · · 1
Chapter 2	My Mother's Secret · · · · · · · · · · · · · · · · · · · 3
Chapter 3	My Background and Family History · · · · · · · · · · · 9
Chapter 4	Trouble in Ogoniland · · · · · · · · · · · · · · · · · 15
Chapter 5	Life in a Corrupt Nigeria · · · · · · · · · · · · · · · 19
Chapter 6	My Journey Begins · · · · · · · · · · · · · · · · · · · 21
Chapter 7	Casualties of Fate · · · · · · · · · · · · · · · · · · · 31
Chapter 8	The Lady Called Alice · · · · · · · · · · · · · · · · · 35
Chapter 9	Alice and the Story of Her Journey to Europe · · · 43
Chapter 10	Initiation into the Business of "Piloting" · · · · · · · 49
Chapter 11	Opportunity Missed · · · · · · · · · · · · · · · · · · · 59
Chapter 12	Desperation—My Exit Attempt at Bamako · · · · · 65
Chapter 13	Departure from Dakar—Perils of the Sea · · · · · · 69
Chapter 14	Apprehended! · 83
Chapter 15	"Promoted" to Ad Hoc Sailor · · · · · · · · · · · · · 87
Chapter 16	The Ghosts of *La Lisa*—1 · · · · · · · · · · · · · · · 91
Chapter 17	The Ghosts of *La Lisa*—2 · · · · · · · · · · · · · · · 93
Chapter 18	Land Ho! · 95
Chapter 19	Curaçao, Netherlands Antilles · · · · · · · · · · · · · 97
Chapter 20	Hostage at the *La Lisa* Iron Prison Cell · · · · · · · 99

Chapter 21	Escape from the *La Lisa* Iron Prison	101
Chapter 22	Hide-and-Seek at the Seaport Harbor	103
Chapter 23	Miracle in Curaçao	109
Chapter 24	Life in the Foreigners' Barracks	115
Chapter 25	Back and Forth with Curaçao Immigration	117
Chapter 26	Riot at the Foreigners' Barracks	123
Chapter 27	My Lawyer Reappears	129
Chapter 28	An Appointment with the Court of Law	131
Chapter 29	My Day in Court	135
Chapter 30	Awaiting Deportation from Curaçao	143
Chapter 31	Arrival of the White Jeep	147
Chapter 32	Freedom!	151
Chapter 33	The Agony of Work without Work Permit	159
Chapter 34	Sad News from Dakar	163
Chapter 35	Tales of Woe from Nigeria	169
Chapter 36	Finally, I Travel to Europe!	175
Chapter 37	The Fate of Foreigners' Barracks	183
Chapter 38	A Visit to Nigeria	187
Chapter 39	A New Nigeria Is Possible	191
Chapter 40	A Word to the Endangered Youth of the World	195

Acknowledgments · 201

CHAPTER 1

An Unusual Childhood

MY NAME IS JERRY ANYAENE.

I was born in the city of Aba, Abia State in Nigeria, West Africa. According to Wikipedia, "Abia is a state in the southeastern part of Nigeria. The capital city is Umuahia, and the major commercial city is Aba, which was formerly a British colonial government outpost in the region. It is also one of the most populated areas in Nigeria. Abia State was created in 1991 from part of Imo State. It is one of the constituent states of the Niger Delta region. It is also the fifth most industrialized state in the country," with a population of over four million.[1]

Abia is mainly peopled by the Igbo ethnic group. Up to 95 percent of the population is Igbo people. Their traditional language is Igbo, and it is in widespread use. English is also widely spoken and serves as the official language in governance and business.

I would like to start off my story by telling you a little about myself and the large family I come from, and about the village, and the city wherein I once lived in Nigeria before I came to Senegal. Yes, I did also live in Dakar, the capital of Senegal, a West African county, many years ago.

---

[1] "Abia State," Wikimedia Foundation, last modified September 27, 2021, 19:50, https://en.wikipedia.org/wiki/Abia_State.

I had some challenges as a child growing up. I wasn't able to do some things that children of my age could easily do. When I was about eight months old, my parents said they were so worried and scared because I hardly cried as a baby. My mother said that any spot she left me to play while she went on her errands would be the same spot I would be at when she came back. I never disturbed anyone or cried for food. She would sometimes smack me on my butt just to make me cry, but I wouldn't. I never struggled to stand on my feet, nor did I try to climb up and down as other children. I was totally fine as I was—just a strange baby who appeared to be in no hurry to do what regular children do, my mother said.

Truly, there was something that set me apart from my family. I always felt that I was being watched and that I was not alone. I realized long ago something that I cannot describe. Words, they say, are very powerful. You can brighten someone's day by what you say to them, and you can hurt someone by what you say.

I also noticed a heightened ability to predict the future. Sometimes I woke up with unpleasant emotions and spoke negatively about a situation, and it would become effective almost immediately, and that scared me. It taught me a valuable lesson on the need to control my thoughts and my words. During my teenage years, I encountered things often in my dreams that came to pass in real life. On many occasions, I saw things before they happened; some I could stop with prayer and petition to God, and some couldn't be stopped. In a nutshell, this was my experience as a child.

CHAPTER 2

My Mother's Secret

I WAS BORN WITH A spiritual gift of the ability to dream and interpret dreams. Like Joseph in the Bible, I dream a lot, and my dreams are often prophetic. This is a very special part of my daily life. Many of my dreams usually come true. When I was seven or eight years old, I had this particular dream, and I woke up the next day and told it to my parents. In that dream, I was standing in front of our building, which was facing a football field, and suddenly a mighty sea started growing inside the football field. Little by little, it became a big ocean, and the waves kept building up and crashing down. It was a very scary spectacle in that dream. I looked to my right hand, and there was this big ship coming toward me in the dream. I then found myself aboard the ship playing with the ship captain's kids.

Suddenly there was a fight on the vessel. People were running up and down, and the captain held me and threw me inside a cell on the ship. His kids started crying, asking their father to let me go, but their father refused. Then, out of nowhere, a white lady appeared and asked the captain to let me go, and he did. In the dream, I went away with the woman and got married to her, and she was so beautiful—tall and slim—and she became pregnant and had kids for me in that dream. When I woke up from that dream as a little child, I was confused, but I clearly remembered all that happened. I quickly ran to my parents and told them about my dream. My father was shocked and speechless. Though he had no interpretation for the dream, he did remind me of something that I'll always have to live with.

Among all my siblings, I was the only one he gave a pet name because he believed that I was special. He always called me by my pet name whenever he was in a good mood or when I did something that impressed him. He always said to me, "Son, I'm just your carnal father on the earth." And he would go on to tell me that I came from a planet called Jovial Planet. I honestly never knew what he was talking about and wondered then in my childish mind if my dad knew me before I was born.

In my hometown, Aba, there are lots of spiritual churches in every location. One afternoon, in my adulthood, I accompanied my girlfriend to her church. The head of their church was an old woman with whitish-gray hair. I never knew that particular place existed until that very day.

To my greatest surprise, while we were inside the church and service was going on, the old woman turned around, looked at me, and pointed to me where I was sitting. She called me "son of a great one" and asked me, "Where is your mother? Is she still alive?"

I answered, "Yes, she's alive" and added, "Please, who are you to her?"

The old woman said to me, "What I'm about to tell you is bigger than you."

She told me I should go home and tell my mother that I had seen the fearless, spiritual old woman with whitish-gray hair. She then asked me to come back with my mom. Immediately I left with my girlfriend and went home to search for my mother. At this time, I no longer lived with them. I had my own apartment. When I found my mother, I told her that I went to a church somewhere in the city and met this old woman who was saying things I wasn't able to understand. I continued, "Please come with me, and tell me if you know or recognize that old woman who claims to know so much about me." My mother was also a prayer warrior in her church, and anything about God excited her. She didn't hesitate to go with me.

We jumped into a taxi, got on the road, and went to see the old woman. We got there, walked into the church, and the very moment my mom saw the gray-haired old woman, she screamed so loud—as if she had seen a ghost. My mother felt so emotional and said, "Oh my God! Oh my God!" The last time they met each other was twenty-two years ago.

I stood outside looking at both of them, trying to understand what was going on. Then, the old woman began telling the story of my life in front of my loving mother.

The old woman said, many years ago, my mother was pregnant, and I, Jerry, was the one in her womb. There was, however, a strange situation that my mother was facing with this pregnancy. My mom, being a Christian woman, was so much into spiritual things and believed in prophecy. In the church where my mom worshiped in my hometown, it had been prophesied to her that she would not live to see the child in her womb—that she had made a promise to this effect in the spiritual world before she was born into the physical world.

Her promise was that on the day of her labor, she would die while giving birth to her fourth child and return to the spiritual world where she came from. My mom is a powerful prayer woman and a believer. When she got that prophecy, she rejected it immediately and denounced the message. She said she had never made such promises to anyone, and neither did she know anything about a past life in the spiritual world. My mother said over and over, by the blood of Jesus Christ, that she would not die and that her unborn child would not die as well. She said she would live to celebrate her child and would live a long life on earth with all her children in this world.

That prophecy gave her sleepless nights, with nightmares after nightmares, day and night. She was totally disorganized because she believed in prophecies as a Christian. She began to visit different churches, holy and unholy, looking for solutions to her problems. Strangely, every church she visited had the same prophecy for her, but she was not accepting it and kept pressing on. No one appeared to have an answer or solution to her problems. She was so scared of losing her life and the life of her unborn child.

She had only a few days before she would go into labor, and she was so traumatized. Luckily, a friend of hers came to see her, and as they talked, she told her about the gray-haired old woman's church. She said the old woman was a seer, and that she prophesied and also had spiritual eyes. When my mother heard all about the old woman, she quickly ran to her church, and the old woman received her warmly but still gave her the same prophecy.

This time, however, she also gave her a solution to her problems. She performed spiritual work on my mom and made her sleep for three days in her church, while she too did three days of dry fasting and prayed over the situation. On the last day of their prayer, she said to my mother, "Go home, madame. God has answered your prayer. Your problems are over; you and your unborn child will live to tell this great testimony someday."

My mother hesitated and said, "I should go?"

The old woman responded, "Yes! Your unborn child and you will not die, says the Lord of Hosts."

The old woman then told my mom that on her labor day, she would see a strange sign and encounter a lot of pain, to the glory of God, and that she would come out as a happy woman. After that day, my mother went to the hospital and went into labor. The gates of hell opened to swallow her and her unborn child. My mother was fighting for her life, and the hospital was fighting to save a child. The nurses and doctor were telling my mother, "Madam, push, push!" However, instead of my mother pushing the baby out, blood kept flowing out.

The nurses who were with her were confused and had to use a small white plastic bucket to carry her blood away. She bled terribly that day. The hospital staff were in shock and confusion, as they were not prepared for such a situation. They considered it a miracle that she was even still alive at that moment. My mom has quite a fighting spirit.

She shouted, "Blood of Jesus!" and immediately pushed me out, with blood covering the baby all over, to God be the glory. Both mother and the baby survived the ordeal. Our God is good.

One week after my birth, my mom took me to visit the old woman at her church to thank the good Lord for a job well done. The old woman was so happy to receive us. She prayed for me and said, "Welcome to the earth." That was the last time my mother saw the old woman.

No one in my family knew about this incident. My parents deliberately kept the story away from me. I don't know the reason why, but I believe the day I met the old woman was the right time for Jehovah God Almighty to reveal to me how I came into the world. It is still a mystery to me how she could remember me after twenty-two years.

When the old woman finished her story, I felt so grateful to my mother for all that she went through just to see that I survived in the land of the living. My eyes were filled with tears of joy, and my mother lowered her head and cried.

My mom said, "Son, I am sorry that we kept this story away from you for so long. But what the old woman said here today was the true story of how you were born." She also said, "I didn't know that the old woman was still living and would be able to recognize you after twenty-two years. God is indeed powerful in his own way." I have often been lost in thought ever since I heard that story.

CHAPTER 3

My Background and Family History

I GREW UP IN MY father's house and knew my father as a police officer. My father, Humphrey Odili Chukwu Anyaene, was born in 1933 in the village of Ndikelionwu in Anambra State, Nigeria.

Geographically, Ndikelionwu is located in Southeast Nigeria, under the current Orumba North Local Government Area. "It is a region with markedly fertile land for agriculture, and with notable prominent products such as rice, yam, cassava, and palm oil. Most of the population are subsistence farmers and traders. There is also a large student community as a result of the presence of a Federal Polytechnic located at Okoh."[2]

Ndikelionwu Local Government Area is a community made up of eleven villages with an estimated population of about 4,200 "situated along the Ekwulobia-Oko-Ufuma-Ajalli-Umunze road. It occupies the land and water areas, bounded in the north by

---

[2] "Orumba North," Wikimedia Foundation, last modified April 16, 2021, 14:44, https://en.wikipedia.org/wiki/Orumba_North.

Ndiowu and Oko town, in the south by Awgbu town, in the east by Ufuma town, and in the west by Nanka town."³

My father was the second of seven children of his father. He started life in very humble circumstances. This is coupled with the facts that he lost his father at a very young age and that his senior brother died soon afterward. Life wasn't easy for him as a child. He needed to work to take care of himself and his siblings.

He left Ndikelionwu at the age of twenty-seven and went to Aba, Abia State, to live there with some of his village relatives.

A couple of years later, he left Aba to struggle in Jos, a cold state in the northern part of Nigeria. In Jos, he went into business, and after some time, he prospered as a trader.

When my father decided it was time to have a family, he went back to his hometown to look for a wife and eventually found this tall, elegant, and beautiful eighteen-year-old girl, Joy Anyaorah, and married her.

In 1963, they had their first son, Kess Odili Chukwu. A few years later, they had another son called Marvelous, and then their third son—me (Jerry). The Nigerian Biafra Civil War started soon after and stalled his life; he lost everything he had acquired in Jos. As he was an Igbo man, going back to Jos at that time would have been sheer suicide; my father stayed put in the village throughout the war. When the war ended in 1970, my father decided to move back to Aba to start all over again. Again, he prospered in trading. My father enlisted in the police force for twenty-eight years in Aba, and things went well for him. A business friend of his convinced him to invest with them in the importation of stockfish. He sold his properties and invested in this business, but it was a scam. My

---

3 "Ndikelionwu, Facts and Fictions—Location," Suplux Media Production, https://ndikelionwu.tripod.com/our-location.html.

father had fallen into the hands of con artists. He once again lost the bulk of his wealth and needed to start all over again.

Despite the mishaps, my father went on to have seven other children. My parents had ten children: five boys and five girls. I am the fourth child.

My father had only one wife, which is my mother, Deaconess Joy Anyaene. However, in Africa, mostly in Nigeria, a man may traditionally marry as many wives as he desires once he can fulfill his obligations to them as their husband, and father of their children. This was common practice many decades ago, though some rich men still marry more than one woman in this generation.

My grandfather from my mother's side married three wives, and he had thirteen daughters, seven sons, and eighty-two grandchildren. My grandfather was well known in my village of Ndikelionwu and had a popular native title, Chief Okwuanasoanya, which means "a noble voice one should respect." He had one of the biggest farms in our village and a lot of acres of land with a large plantation. One of his lands contained a small river called Mirinwanma, which means "the beautiful river." This river is inside a forest just ten minutes away from our home in the village. The road that leads to this river is very narrow and is flanked on both sides by a lot of palm trees and coconut trees.

Some people go there in the middle of the night to get clean water. They would carry their lamps and flashlights to see the road clearly because of the darkness. I usually go there to fetch drinking water for the family during December periods when we visited the village. Once, our family visited the village and arrived very late in the night during the Christmas holidays. Unfortunately, we had run out of drinking water, and there was no electricity in the village—it was totally dark.

My elder brother decided to go and fetch some water from the river. I heard my mom say to him, "No, son, it's too late," but he had already made up his mind to go. He was accompanied by one of my brothers; they carried their lamp and flashlight. On their way to the river, a wild pig with horns came out from nowhere and chased after them. They ran for their lives and threw away their lamp and flashlight while running in the darkness. My elder brother was crying and shouting, "Mommy, Mommy." It was so fearful that night. We thanked God they made it home safe.

The river has a natural phenomenon that forbade people from swimming or taking baths in it. If you swam or took a bath in it, the river would change its color from clear to a yellow hue, and once this is noticed, no one could fetch drinking water there until the next day. The river appeared to love cleanliness—and that's why they call it the beautiful river. Everyone loved to go there for fresh and clean drinking water.

My grandfather was a well-known palm oil producer and exporter in our village and in other neighboring villages. He was once partially pronounced dead at his home for over nine hours in 1999 and later came back to life, started throwing up, and vomited a small live catfish out of his mouth. According to native beliefs, such an occurrence was an indication that he had been poisoned by a member of his own family. He then accused one of his wives and her children who he said wanted him dead so they could have access to all his lands with large plantations in them.

My grandfather later died in 2009 at the age of 107, broken-hearted, because he lost some of his daughters as well as his first and second sons from his first wife.

There was contention over his property after he died because he did not want to leave any of his inheritance to his children, since they neglected him in his old age. Also, the children did not want the grandchildren to take the inheritance.

After my grandfather passed away, a few years later my grandmother too passed away, and she was the first wife. The male children of the second and third wife then decided to share the inheritance among themselves, since my grandmother (his first wife) had lost two of her sons before she passed away. So, not even my mother and her sisters could get any part of his inheritance.

At a young age, my father, Humphrey Anyaene, was transferred from Aba to Ogoniland in Nigeria as a police officer, and some of the family members went with him.

Ogoniland is located "in the Rivers South East senatorial district of Rivers State, in the Niger Delta region of southern Nigeria." The Ogoni population is over two million people. They live on approximately 404 square miles, or 1,050 square kilometers, of land east and southeast of Port Harcourt in Rivers State, Nigeria.[4]

There are six native languages spoken by the Ogoni people. According to Wikipedia, "the largest is Khana, the dialects of the six kingdoms, Gokana, Tae (Tẹẹ), Eleme, and Baen Ogoi."[5] Their language is very interesting and sweet to hear when they interact with each other. As a child, I found it difficult to speak new languages. Even my own native language was a challenge to me. Sometimes my father would chase me out of the house for pronouncing things incorrectly in Igbo. I was, however, able to communicate in broken English, and only my elder brother out of all my siblings spoke a little of it.

---

4 "Ogoni people," Wikimedia Foundation, last modified September 20, 2021, 14:15, https://en.wikipedia.org/wiki/Ogoni_people.

5 "Ogoni people."

CHAPTER 4

Trouble in Ogoniland

WE LIVED IN OGONILAND FOR a few years before my father decided to move back to the city of Aba, Abia State, because of the violence and kidnappings there.

The people of Ogoniland had been victims of violence for years. Most of the world know that the people of Ogoni had been denied their basic human rights for many years, and that our Nigerian government kept quiet and did nothing to redress the situation.

The origin of the Ogoni problem of the Ijaw people of the Niger Delta was the discovery of oil in their land. Shell Oil Company had been drilling it for many years. My father told me that Shell discovered oil in Ogoni in 1955.

To this day, they have taken untold millions of barrels of crude oil from the wells of Ogoniland that are worth billions upon billions of dollars.

None of this money was used for the development of the villages of the Ogoni people. With the high-pressure oil and dirty gas, the entire village was polluted, and many died by inhaling toxic gas. The village river became colored, and oil spills were everywhere. It was so polluted that one could barely get clean water to drink.

There were too many promises from the government that were never kept. These promises were easily broken, and due to the prevailing nature of government at the time, no one dared say anything for fear of military backlash.

Consequently, the poor village of Ogoni kept on suffering every day from the polluted air and toxic gases.

One early morning in 1993, the Ogoni community started protesting against Shell. It was a sad day and an unhappy protest. The Nigerian security force that was guarding Shell's facilities tried to stop some people who were protesting close to their gate.

Somehow violence started. Some people threw bottles and stones. Shell closed its gate and called for more security men. Every day for many years, the people of Ogoni protested against Shell because of the promises that were not kept.

The corrupt government of Nigeria kept silent about the Ogoni people's demand until 1996, when the violence became worse. That was when the Nigerian government woke up. One night in 1997, Nigerian troops invaded the entire village without notice.

Immediately, they started holding the villagers hostage and killed people, including some missionaries who came from Eastern Europe.

Unfortunately, the government dissolved the office that my father was working in because they took part in the protest against the corrupt politicians who controlled the entire village.

I believe my father was a senior police officer at that time because I remember as a young boy seeing a group of police officers parked in their police van driving to my house just to pick up my father every morning. He would sit in the front of the car taking salutes from his boys—the lower-rank police officers.

He lost his younger brother, a police inspector, in the deadly violence that followed the invasion of Ogoni village. My dad lost his job and was afraid for his life and his family. So far, he had been in the Nigerian police force for over twenty-eight years. I also knew him as one who feared the Lord.

My father had always wanted to serve God, and that was what he did following his exit from the police force. He delved deep into church activities. He traveled around preaching the Word of God, and dedicated most of his life to the service of God and humanity. He passed away on July 15, 2019, at the age of eighty-six.

CHAPTER 5

Life in a Corrupt Nigeria

WHEN WE MOVED BACK TO Aba, life there was awfully hard and miserable.

In Nigeria, many people struggle to survive despite the fact that Nigeria is a resource-rich country and that, expectedly, the opposite should be the case.

Nigeria is one of the most populous countries in West Africa and one of the world's major oil producers. However, our politicians and leaders have been destroying the nation through the introduction of the culture of extravagant lifestyles to the citizenry, thereby luring them into the mindset that money is everything and hard work and honesty are nothing. The typical Nigerian politician is a greedy hypocrite who does not care about the citizens of the country.

Before these greedy politicians get into power, they promise heaven and earth to the citizens, when, in fact, their major objective is just to steal the country's wealth. Most foreign companies and foreign leaders have also helped to corrupt Nigerian leaders and politicians.

When our leaders steal Nigeria's wealth and oil money, foreign governments help them to keep all that money in their country for their own interests. It would have been a good thing if our leaders used all the billions of dollars they stole from our country to develop our nation and help the poor.

Instead, our leaders steal all this money, and take it to Europe or to one of the Caribbean nations for themselves and their families. These corrupt foreign nations, some of which do not have much natural resources, then use this money to develop their own countries. Some of these nations are Switzerland, Germany, the United States, the United Kingdom, Italy, France, and many more of them.

The truth is that many of these foreign countries are selfish and greedy. They punish corruption in their government systems but encourage it in developing Third World nations. Foreign governments ought to ensure that policies are put in place to prevent political leaders of developing nations from stashing their corrupt and bloody money in their banks.

When something happens to one of these Nigerian leaders or politicians, they never get this money back from the foreign countries. Usually, when they die, not even a family member can claim all this money that they hid overseas.

Honestly, corruption in Nigeria will never stop unless Nigerians get rid of all the corrupt leaders who we still have today. Other African countries must do the same: get rid of their corrupt leaders.

That will be the only way to solve the problems that the African people are facing today.

General Ibrahim Babangida's regime fueled the present problems that Nigeria is facing today. From 1985 to 1993, corruption was widespread during his regime. This is what gave birth to the present-day predicament of Nigeria. Most Nigerians, if not all, wonder why Babangida is walking about as a free man in Nigeria today, still exerting subtle control, though remotely, over governmental affairs.

CHAPTER 6

My Journey Begins

I HAD TO RUN FOR dear life because of the fighting, killings, and kidnappings in my hometown.

Life in Nigeria was hard too. There were no jobs, and the level of corruption in the nation was just too much. Some criminals had taken advantage of the region's instability to make money from kidnappings and to demand for ransoms from the oil companies they believed were stealing the country's oil.

Kidnapping became too much of a problem because those doing it had turned it into a lucrative business. The situation degenerated to the point where even people who knew nothing about the looting of the nation's resources—law-abiding citizens—were regularly victimized. It became obvious that the soil of Nigeria could not allow the seed of my destiny and ambitions to grow and flourish. It was time to leave.

I left Nigeria and went to the Republic of Benin, another African country. I stayed there for a few weeks, and I did some concierge work to get money while I was there. The ultimate goal of my journey was to get to Europe for the hope of a better life.

I took a bus, and it took me ten days to pass through the following countries: the Republic of Benin, Burkina Faso, Ghana, Côte D'Ivoire, and Mali. The bus I took went through the villages to get to Bamako, the capital of Mali. I was fired by the thoughts of making a better life for myself so as to enable me to send money back home to my brothers, sisters, and parents, to support with their upkeep. The condition of my family was very bad since my father lost his job as a police officer. He was no longer able to help his family move forward. My mom was not doing better as well. My sisters and brothers had already dropped out of school, since there was no money to pay for their schooling. To eat three square meals in a day was a huge task. Life was indeed quite miserable for us.

When I got to Bamako, I took a train to Senegal. I remember that while I was trying to locate the train station, a group of kids aged from eight to nine years were loitering around me. They suddenly grabbed me and tried to cut my pocket to take my money. Fortunately, I had no money in my pocket. I had learned that the safer place to keep money was in one's underwear.

I took a train to Dakar, the capital of Senegal. It was more beautiful than all the other countries I had passed on my way. Our train arrived in the night, and I was quite surprised and thought I was in Europe already. There were a lot of white French men and ladies on the streets. The city is beautiful and full of life. Everywhere looked amazing, with tall buildings, streetlights, big hotels, casinos, and clubhouses scattered here and there. It was a long journey to get to Dakar. I took a moment and sat down at a corner of the train station and had some delicious local street food.

My purpose for going to Senegal was to get to a place called Tangier in Morocco. From there, I could travel to Europe on a boat. Upon arrival in Senegal, I spent a night in the Dakar Motor Park. I thought it would be easy to travel from Senegal to Europe, but it was more difficult than I thought. I wished I could travel by air, but that was not possible because I needed a visa and more money, which I didn't have.

So, with the little money I had left, I set out to look for a place to stay in Dakar. I left the park to go into the city to check it out. However, my bag was still somewhere in the park, in a safe spot where I hid it. I took a random bus into the city, not knowing where to go. I was sad because I had forgotten the name of the park buildings, and their names were in French.

Virtually everyone in Dakar spoke French and Wolof, and the only language I knew was English. I'd been told that one of my uncles, Chika, was living in Senegal, but nobody in my mother's family knew where he was living. He had been away for over twenty-eight years. The last time I saw him, before he left Nigeria, I was ten years old. When I remembered he was in Senegal, I decided that was the time to look for him, which was funny, because Senegal is too big to look for someone without knowing their address.

While I was searching for a place to stay, I met two Nigerians, Kenneth and Ifeanyi, who owned a barbershop in Dakar. I told both of them I'd run out of Nigeria because of too much violence; it was horrible.

Kenneth told me that thousands of Africans were in Senegal to travel to Europe, but it wasn't so easy to leave Dakar to go to Europe.

I told them I would stay for a while. They started laughing and asked me if I still had some money with me, and I said yes.

They told me the best thing to do was to buy my train ticket back to Nigeria because Senegal was a hard place to live. Both of them had been living in Dakar for twelve years; they also came to Senegal to travel to Europe. They couldn't make it, and it wasn't at all easy to continue with their journey, so the two of them opened up a barbershop.

Kenneth told me there were eighteen of them who came to Dakar; some people couldn't face the hard life. They met a Portuguese man who offered some of them illegal drug business, and they left Dakar to join the business.

There was an incident in which a few of those people died in the high sea along with thirty-eight other young people on a fisher's boat going to Spain. Many Africans choose to take on the massive risk in the high sea because of the nature of the problems faced every day in Africa. They all preferred to take the risk to go to Europe in order to seek a better future.

After two weeks, another person who was sent by the same Portuguese man to bring drugs to China died in a Chinese airport when the swallowed illicit drugs in his stomach burst open.

When Kenneth finished telling their story, I slipped into a sea of sadness. I became more upset mainly because generally, Africans facing adverse situations usually believe that their brighter future lies in Europe. This was the case with me, of course. Ifeanyi told me that this was my best opportunity to go back to Nigeria before the little money I had ran out. But I had no other choice than to stay for a while. I had come too far to go back now. My feet had walked through the mountains and the desert to get to Dakar. In my mind, there was no hope for happiness back home in Nigeria—a nation filled with broken promises from soulless leaders with no one to hold them accountable, violence, crime, and hunger—a nation saturated with sorrow and fear, and needless deaths. No, there was no going back. I had gotten too far to go back.

Kenneth advised me to save the money I had with me, asking me what I was doing in the motor park and reminding me of its name. The only thing I could remember was that it was close to the sea. It took me four and a half hours to locate the park; it was one heck of a day.

I went back to the salon with my bag. Kenneth and Ifeanyi allowed me to sleep in their salon, where they had been working and living for years.

I asked Kenneth if he knew any Nigerian who lived in Dakar called Chika, but he said that in Dakar, there were many people with the name Chika.

Well, I said, the one I was asking about was from Ndikelionwu village. Immediately he called my uncle by his native name, and he said he knew him.

I asked Kenneth to take me to my uncle's house, but he refused and started laughing at me.

He said, "Hey, Mr. Man, we don't know who you are or where you're coming from. Are you sure he is your uncle? Look at the time; it is late." It was 10:45 p.m. "It looks like you don't know him—you don't even know his address."

"It is the truth," I insisted. I only knew him when I was ten years old. But I believed that if I saw him, I would recognize him. I spent the night in their barber salon.

The next day Kenneth went to look for my uncle, and he told me he would not go with me, that maybe my uncle would not remember me. It had been a long time since he left Nigeria.

A couple of hours later, Kenneth came back alone and said, "Your uncle did not believe the story I told him—he felt you might be a ghost." I was sad, though he told me not to be worried, as Uncle Chika was coming.

Later that evening, my uncle came into the salon. I was both thrilled and amazed to see that he looked just the same. My uncle couldn't believe his eyes. He thought he saw a ghost and said, "Boy, you look exactly like my older sister." My mother and I both looked alike. He then started crying, not because I found him but because it had been so long he had seen me. I remembered I was ten years old when he left Nigeria. He took my bag, and we went to his house.

My uncle's wife was happy to see me. She welcomed me into their house. She stated she'd been wishing to meet the members of her husband's family.

I started living with my uncle, his wife, and his kids in Dakar. My uncle had gotten married to a Senegalese woman, with none of my mother's family in Nigeria knowing about the marriage.

It was very difficult for me to find a job. First, I needed to learn how to speak French and the native language, Wolof. My uncle's kids started teaching me how to speak French so I could communicate with the people in Dakar.

One evening, I went to a club to have a good time. It was a French club, and I hoped they spoke English. The club was full of white people, and they had one big and strong security guard, a man with big muscles, at the gate—the bouncer. I was marveled by the appearance of the security man. I had never seen someone as physically built as he was. He was my uncle's neighbor, and he spoke a little English.

The security man let me inside the club. We packed in with French and Lebanese people. The club was beautiful, though everyone there spoke French. There is one thing about the French clubs in Dakar: their ladies are always in a good mood and ready to have a good time with you, but you must speak French.

One Saturday evening, I went back to the same club without knowing that the first day I came there, a French lady had been staring at me. But this time, I noticed her, and she smiled at me. I smiled back. Her name was Kate, and her father was in one of the French mafias in Dakar. Where I sat that day, there was no sign that anyone was looking at me, but her father was in the club with a Lebanese and Senegalese drug cartel leader.

I was sitting inside with the security man. She walked to me and asked my name in French, and she started speaking with me in French; I didn't know what she was talking about.

I told her I spoke English, and she was still willing to talk to me. Then I asked the security man to help me out because he was a Senegalese man who spoke French.

I thought I had found a new friend, without knowing that the security man would cause problems for me. He had been nursing feelings for the lady for a very long time.

Kate spoke to the security man, and she wrote her information down for me.

She gave me 400 US dollars, which was a lot of money, 280,000 CFA francs, and ordered a couple of drinks for us and left the club. The man walked out, refusing to give me the information Kate wrote for me. He wouldn't communicate with me.

A week later, I went back to the club to search for Kate. This time I was a bit more wary of the security man because he was the club bouncer. I went to him as usual, and he was unhappy to see me. Kate passed by me and acted as if she didn't see me. She went straight to her friends to hang out and drink. I guessed she was upset with me. I tried to communicate with her in French. Oh boy! I felt so disappointed I couldn't express myself in French. I was sweating.

While I was still trying to explain what happened, one of her friends stood up. She spoke English. "You were invited over to her father's house?" They had been expecting me, but I never showed up. I heard Kate, with a low voice, say, "Au revoir."

The next morning, the security man went to my uncle's wife and told her I wanted to destroy his dream. He'd been working in that club for nine years and known that French lady for four years. Oh, the man had a secret crush on her, but he didn't know how to communicate with her. He said he talked to her a long time ago, but she refused to respond to him. My uncle's wife pleaded with me to forget the club and the lady, which I did. I later got a job in a fashion company as a designer. The company belonged to a Senegalese man; my uncle's wife got the job for me.

When I began working there, I started speaking a little French. Only the owner spoke French there, while the rest spoke Wolof. We had six designers in that fashion house. It was a surprise to me that I was the only one among them who could speak a little French. They all spoke their native language—Wolof. Communication was poor between us, and I started becoming restless. I felt I couldn't work there any longer because I discovered that it was jeopardizing my dream of going to Europe.

I quit the job without telling them the reason. It was simply too much hard work to explain my reason in French. I told my uncle that I was planning to go to Europe and that this was the reason I came to Senegal. My uncle was not against the idea. It was apparently the dream of most African people, rich or poor. He, however, advised me to consider the risk of going to Europe with no one helping me. He said that for now, he had no money to support my plans.

He was sorry that he was not there in Nigeria to teach me how to be a man. He knew I could face any responsibility that came my way, and he also knew that our family in Nigeria was facing serious issues with no one helping them to stand on their feet. He repeated that he would have loved to support me, but that it was very hard for him to support his own family in Senegal.

My uncle's wife also told me that traveling to Europe was a very important thing in an African man's life. She said that if she had money, she would have helped me go there to work and live. She said I could see how things were with them—that they found it hard to feed, and that my uncle had lost his business a long time ago.

She said that the only way I could go to Europe was by boat, but they would never support it or approve of it because many people died on the high seas just to be in Europe. She wanted me to return to work where she'd found a job for me, but I never went back there again.

My uncle and his wife had smoking issues, and sometimes I worried about their lifestyle. If I had money, I would have found another place to live.

When I came to Senegal, I was planning to stay only for a little while, but before I knew it, two years had already passed without any step being taken in the direction of Europe. While I was in

Dakar, I surmised that Dakar was not the best transit location for Africans who wanted to go to Europe. It seemed that once you arrived and decided to stay a little while, you would never leave again without someone helping you.

Senegal was a transit hub for many Africans who were trying to travel to Europe by road or by sea. Of those who attempted to travel to Europe, some of them made it, while some ended up living in Senegal. Some also died there and were buried there.

CHAPTER 7

Casualties of Fate

IT WAS A MIRACLE THAT I found my uncle in Senegal, and I wished I could tell my parents that I saw him in Dakar. For over eighteen years, they had never seen him or heard from him. However, there was no way for me to communicate with my parents in Nigeria. We had no phone in our house for communication from the time I left Nigeria to travel to Senegal in 1997 to the year 2000. Therefore, my parents did not know that I had left Nigeria to travel to other African countries by road. No one knew where I was. My mother did have a feeling that I might be planning to leave the city, but she was not sure where I was going. My parents did not hear from me for a very long time while I was in those other African countries.

I would have sent a letter to my parents so they would know where I was, but it might have taken five to ten years before they would have gotten it, or it might have gotten lost on the way. For you to receive a letter in Nigeria, you might need to have a safe box in a post office. You could also receive letters when you were living in the city, but where my parents were living, the post office did not send letters.

Dakar is a beautiful place to live, but not for the Africans who are trying to travel to Europe by boat and by road. That night, I left my uncle's house without telling anyone. I was becoming more and more worried that I would never leave Senegal.

I came back the next day, and my uncle started asking me about my plans in Dakar, if I still wanted to stay with them in Senegal. My uncle told me he had friends who worked at Dakar's seaport. He told me they might help to put me on board, but he would never do that because it would be too risky, and I was his nephew.

I begged him to take me to his friends who were working at the seaport, but he refused. I was only staying in his house doing nothing; there was nothing to do in Senegal. Every day I went back to the barbershop and hooked up with some African guys who had nothing to do from morning to night. That was not the life I wanted to live.

All the Africans who came to Senegal to travel to Europe stayed there. Over eleven people, mostly Nigerian, were sleeping in one salon, and none of these guys had any money to support themselves.

To get food in Dakar was an enormous problem for many people, especially migrants. Some of those who were sleeping inside the salon would eat nothing in the morning, eating only in the afternoon when the owner of the salon bought food. Every afternoon, all these guys would run back to the salon just to eat, and over eleven guys would eat from one plate.

If any of them came in late, he would eat nothing until the next afternoon because they didn't have any money with them. They all came to Dakar to travel by boat to Europe, but unfortunately, not all of them would make it.

One day we were in church, and some Dakar police officers entered and asked the whole church to come outside. The police officers asked us to come to the seashore to see if we could identify dead Africans pulled from the sea.

I was there watching the entire process, which was a sad moment for the whole church. The reason the police came to us was that some of the guys had Nigerian passports with them.

Police officers were turning over their bodies to see if we could recognize any of them. Six of them had Nigerian passports; the other four didn't have any documents with them. Their parents didn't know that they were dead because most of them had barely arrived in Dakar. What a loss for their families in Nigeria.

I knew two of the dead bodies because I had seen them previously in the salon. The next day, I went back to the salon and told them what I saw on Sunday at the seashore. This was not a comforting news. The news got many scared, and the entire salon became quiet because they knew some of the dead guys. I was so traumatized that I couldn't go to church again because of what I witnessed that Sunday morning. I knew the church would always remind me of the dead guys I had seen lying face down on the sandy beach—all of whom were ambitious young men on their way to Europe for better living conditions; all were formerly bound inextricably to their hopes and dreams, and now they had become casualties of fate.

I went back to my uncle, and asked him to help me, saying that I was tired of staying in Dakar. One afternoon, my uncle took me to one of his Senegalese friends who was working with the coast guard at Dakar's seaport. Had the turning point for me and my quest finally arrived? Only time would tell.

CHAPTER 8

The Lady Called Alice

WHEN WE GOT TO THE seaport, my uncle told his friend that I needed his help, and that I came to Senegal to travel to Europe. His friend asked me if I had any money to pay my fare, and if I had traveled on a boat before, because it wasn't a straightforward journey. The man told me he would contact my uncle if any suitable ships came to Dakar and then he would check if the ships were going to Italy or France. The man also said that most Senegalese people who traveled to Europe go to Italy and France, which were the only contacts he had.

It thrilled me to hear from the man. We spent a little time with him, and then we went back home. One morning, I became very sad because I had waited for months to hear from the coast guard officer who promised to help put me on a ship, but he was nowhere to be seen.

My uncle later told me that the man had left Dakar, and that he didn't know when he would be back. He, however, promised he would look out for more of his friends who worked in the same place.

That morning, a friend of my uncle from our church came to visit us. His name was Austin. Austin had been in Senegal for a very long time. While I was chatting with him, he asked me if I knew the reason why he visited us that morning. Austin asked me if I remembered a certain sister in our local church where we worshiped every Sunday whose name was Alice. Her story was that she initially came to Senegal to travel to Europe, but it was very difficult for her, just like it was for everyone else. Many were of the opinion that of all the African ladies who living in Dakar, Alice was definitely one of the nicest.

Austin said the reason he came to my uncle's house was that Alice sent him to invite me to her home. In the church where I worshiped in Dakar, everyone was pleased with the way God was using me there. I was blessed with spiritual gifts, which included healing, prophecies, and the manifest presence of God during ministration. When I prayed and asked God for his mercies, He always provided it.

The church where we worshiped in Dakar was one of the bigger ones, and Alice was a well-known member. Usually, anytime I saw her in the church, she was always with many ladies around her. A lot of ladies went to that church, and the pastor would pray frequently for them to find kindhearted white men who would take them to Europe.

Though I had not met a lady with whom I wanted to have a committed relationship, I remembered a relationship I had in 1990 in Nigeria. I met this beautiful lady named Chidiebere. My parents liked her so much. We were together for close to a year before we broke off.

One morning, Chidiebere told me she wanted to travel to Port Harcourt, a state in Nigeria, for some business, and that she would be back the next day. Little did I know that this journey would be the beginning of the end for our relationship.

I mentioned earlier that my father was a police officer in the city where I was living in Nigeria; a few police officers who worked with my dad knew that Chidiebere and I were in a relationship. As far as I was aware, she left around eight o'clock in the morning; however, I had not heard from her.

That evening, while I was with some of the police officers in my father's office, a police officer came in and told me they had arrested Chidiebere. I was shocked and surprised. The officer told me they arrested her in the company of a man alone in a school field around 11:55 p.m.

I felt so sad that my parents knew about our relationship. The police officer told me they had taken both of them to the police station, and that they would not get out on bail. He said that it was too late for me to see her that night, but I was still battling to believe that the story he was telling me was real. Chidiebere had left me in the morning for Port Harcourt; that was what she told me, and I always believed her.

I went that night to see things for myself. When I got to the police station, I discovered that the story that the officer told was true. Chidiebere and the mystery man were indeed in detention.

She started crying, saying that she was so sorry and that it was the devil who put her in that situation. Of course, who else to blame? I then asked her about the man whom she was with. The man knew me obviously. It turned out that both of them worked in the same company.

I tried to bail her out of detention that night, but I couldn't. The police officers said they had been given an order that they'd spend the night there. The next day they released both of them.

Now back to Senegal. I asked Austin why Alice had invited me, because in the church where we worshiped, I was not the only young man there. He started telling me about Alice—how she helped many guys in Senegal, and even in the church. Many of the church members depended on her because in Senegal, it was very hard to survive. If one had no outside help, he said, the only people who could help you in Dakar were the Nigerian ladies because most of the Nigerian men in Dakar at the time were doing nothing. He hoped I understood.

I accepted the invitation but wasn't looking for any woman to fall in love with just yet. I simply wanted to leave Senegal. I still had so many dreams to chase, and I had made a promise to myself that I would make no commitment to any lady while I was still in pursuit of my dreams. I was just not prepared to cripple my plans.

Austin told me that back home in Nigeria, he was married and had four boys and two girls. He, however, came to Senegal alone to seek for a way to travel to Europe. He said he had initially arrived in Senegal with my uncle, but that my uncle saw a Senegalese lady, whom he liked and married, and so I should also see Alice and know what I thought of her. Alice spent her money and her time cooking a special meal for us. Indeed, if we did not come that day, she would have been most unhappy with us. It turned out that Austin was also hoping to get some help from her.

Ever since she came to Senegal, she had had no boyfriend, and she didn't want to open up to the church members.

Austin knew what my problem was and so continued piling on the pressure. He told me that Alice knew some sailors who worked on a ship who might help me get on board and take me to Europe. Alice had paid some sailors to take a couple of guys to Europe, and they had arrived successfully.

For that reason alone, I accepted the invitation, and we went to her house. Alice was a nice, kind lady. She asked what I was doing here in Dakar and said that Senegal was not a place where a young man could survive.

I told her I came to Senegal to see if I could get a boat that would take me to Europe.

She looked at me and asked me if I knew how many thousands of Africans died on the high seas every day. She told me my uncle was a generous man, whom she had helped twice with financial problems, and that if I really wanted to go to Europe, she would show me what to do. Once I accepted, I would easily get to Europe.

We spent the entire day together. It thrilled her to meet me, and she promised to see to it that I left Senegal. Within a couple of days, she became my girlfriend.

Austin later left Dakar for Morocco, but I heard that life was horrible for him, and so he went back to Mali and opened up an African restaurant.

My uncle told me that before he got married, he knew Alice and had asked her out on a date. She, however, refused him. I suddenly started having problems with my uncle. He complained about everything that I did in his house. Even in church he complained.

Anytime he saw that I was with Alice, he got jealous, though he was a very sweet man and kind by nature.

The pastor of the church asked me why my uncle was always complaining about me whenever he saw me with Alice. He told me to be sure of what I wanted to do with my life. He had seen quite a number of things within the period he was in Dakar.

On one occasion, while he was in the church, some people came to tell him about what had happened to some church members who left for Europe. The coast guards brought in their bodies, and said that a fisherman caught them with his nets, but they were already dead.

I once heard of a Moroccan man who took lots of money from people, including a pregnant woman, just to take them on his boat. The Moroccan man helped them, but they all died in the high seas, and their bodies floated about in the ocean.

As we continued to talk, he told me that some of his members had actually left that very day. They were on the road to Morocco, which they said would be an easier way for them to get to Spain. The pastor said that he didn't know if they would make it to Europe, and that Alice knew some sailors who could take people aboard their ship and successfully get to Europe.

There were a few other friends from the same church who were trying to get in contact with Alice. I thought I was the only one who was troubled about leaving Dakar.

My uncle's wife worked as a travel agent, and she was the one who supported their family. My uncle said that he lost his previous job but had another business that gave him a little money. He would give information to the navy boats, the coast guard, and the civil guard whom he worked together with to fight the battle against drugs in Dakar.

But I was not happy with the way my uncle acted when he saw me with Alice. I had no other choice than to leave my uncle's house. It was a really hard choice to make.

CHAPTER 9

Alice and the Story of Her Journey to Europe

I STARTED LIVING WITH ALICE, my girlfriend, in Dakar, but I never knew what business she was into. All I can remember is that Nigerian guys in Dakar came to Alice's house to eat and borrow money. She would always give her money to the African people who were stranded in Dakar. Life in Senegal was challenging for so many Africans, and they were ready to do just about anything to survive.

Alice told me about the business she and many African ladies were doing in Senegal. It was very painful to hear. Her family in Nigeria didn't know about it. She said that many African ladies from different countries who came to Dakar were all just looking for a way to travel to Europe—the land of their hopes and dreams. All these ladies went after white men and made their living through legalized prostitution, and she was one of them.

I was both shocked and sad. I thought I'd found a sincere churchgoing lady. She started telling me about herself and her life. Ever since she came to Dakar, she'd been saving money to buy a ticket and a British passport so that she could travel to Europe. But she always ended up using the money to help the church and the African brothers who were stranded in Dakar.

The reason she left Nigeria was that she'd finished her university education but couldn't find employment, so one of her friends taught her what some African ladies in her situation did. They traveled to Europe for a better life.

Life in Nigeria was tough for her family, and no one could help her. She had one daughter, and they locked up the father of her daughter in China for trafficking drugs. She left her daughter with the mother of her boyfriend and went away with the lady who had told her about Europe.

Six of them left Nigeria the same day to travel to Morocco by road. It took them twelve days to get to Morocco's border, but the military at the border sent them to Mali because the two ladies who were with them didn't have their passports.

At all the borders they passed, they paid money to the military to allow them to pass through. Mali was horrible and hot, and within two days, they left Mali and went to Dakar.

When they arrived in Dakar, they had no money left, and they couldn't go any further. She said that they then met four Nigerian guys who were staying at the same hotel. They had come into town to buy motor parts, and Alice and her friends told them their problems. The Nigerian guys responded that they wanted to help them with some money, but would only do so if they agreed to have sex with them. Upset, they rejected the mean-spirited offer.

In the hotel where they stayed, they also met a lady from Zimbabwe. She promptly taught them about the business she and other ladies at the hotel were doing. In Dakar, the life the African ladies were living was considered normal—to be paid to have sex with the white men who were staying there as tourists.

Alice said that the Senegalese ladies had no choice; they always went with any man who offered money to them because of how difficult it was to make a living in Dakar. Other African ladies from different countries learned quickly and did the same thing. She told me that these African ladies never liked to go out with black guys in Senegal, except the ones who came from Europe, America, or an Arab country, because some of them were rich.

She said that they didn't come to Dakar to play around. They left their homes in Nigeria to come to Senegal to see if they could get to Europe (where they hoped to find a better life) on a boat. One day she took a risk and went on the boat, but the day she went on the boat to travel to Europe, the weather was terrible, and their boat came back to Dakar.

The boat's owner didn't refund their money. She said that he was out of his mind because anytime sailors ventured into the ocean, they took drugs to face their fears. She said that she was truly afraid of the maritime weather, and that was why she was still in Senegal.

Prostitution was far from uncommon in Dakar. Most of the prostitutes in Dakar lived with their boyfriends in the same house. Their boyfriends were all black guys, but every night, they would go out to look for white men or sailors. That was the only way they could save money to buy a ticket and an international passport to travel to Europe by air.

There was another group of men from Benin City, a city in Nigeria, who took money from ladies because they had their men as contacts in embassies to procure visas for the ladies, so they could go to Europe for prostitution.

Some of these ladies would get to Europe and would be deported back to Dakar to start all over again. For the Senegalese and other African ladies living in Dakar, prostitution was the only thing they knew. The crazy and stupid thing was that the government of Senegal supported the prostitution that was going on in Dakar. What the government of Senegal did was that they registered all of them at their government hospital, and their actions were not illegal in Senegal.

They all walked around in the clubs and on the road with their prostitution ID card. Without this card, you could not go to the club or work on the road at night to look for a white man or a sailor.

The government of Senegal told the police officers to control them at night, to see if their prostitution ID cards were up-to-date. Most of these ladies slept in jail for not having their prostitution ID cards, and some of them were afraid to go to the Dakar government hospital because of what they had experienced there.

She said every week they had to visit the hospital for checkups and get treatment if they had contracted sexually transmitted diseases. The hospital wouldn't take money from them. They only took their blood, up to one pint of blood, each week they visited the hospital. What Dakar's hospital was doing was exporting their blood to Europe. Alice said the hospital either sold it to France, or they would use it for other purposes. That was the only way the hospital could recoup its expenses from the prostitutes and make a profit.

The craziest thing was that the government obviously knew what the hospital was doing. These ladies couldn't talk to the hospital administration or tell people what they were doing because they were in the prostitution business.

If they didn't go to the hospital while they were on the job, then they would get into enormous problems with the Dakar police officers. The police always checked these ladies at night to see if the hospital signed their cards. If not, they would end up in jail and lose their business for that day.

Many didn't know about what Alice was telling me because I was the only one who was close to her. She said that many of the African ladies who lived in Italy were in the same prostitution business because it was difficult for them to take care of themselves or help their families. There was no good education for the poor ones back in the villages of many African countries—no job and no future for them.

The way things are currently, I am not sure that African leaders have any good plan for the survival or prosperity of future generations. From the outside, you may not understand or feel what people go through. But if you happen to find yourself out there all alone, you will know what it means to struggle for survival.

I know that one way or another, many people have experienced problems in their lives. The peculiarity of Africans is that we have been so traumatized and abused that we are prepared to do all kinds of things just to see that we survive, or drop dead trying.

CHAPTER 10

Initiation into the Business of "Piloting"

WHEN ALICE FINISHED WITH HER story, I felt so sad, and the world seemed so cold to me. Truly, life in Senegal was horrible. Even the cities of Senegal didn't have work for their youths.

The only job that was available in Senegal to them was police job, and most of the youths in Senegal became police officers. My uncle knew the business Alice was doing, and most of the ladies he knew did the same business as her. They were not ashamed of it because it was a normal thing in Dakar for a lady to do.

Oftentimes, the ladies who made it to Europe would continue with the same business of prostitution, and the ones who didn't make it out of Dakar would continue with the same business while they were in Dakar. Some of them would get lucky when they got to Europe and meet a white man who would promise to marry them. Most of those white men who slept with these African ladies while they were in Dakar also took them to Europe if they promised to stop prostituting themselves once they got there.

I had a friend in Dakar named Chukwuma. I didn't know that his girlfriend, Tina, was doing the same business as Alice. One day

Alice took me to Chukwuma's house because there was a party going on there. When we arrived, I found out that Tina was getting married to a white man from London. Tina had met him on the ship.

Tina initially came to Senegal to see if she could travel on a boat to Europe, but it was difficult for her. The coast guard caught her a couple of times, and she ran out of money. She became frustrated in Dakar, and nobody would help her. Tina had no choice but to prostitute herself, and she met Chukwuma.

Chukwuma was outside crying, and the white man was inside drinking with the Africans who came for the party. The man didn't know that Tina was Chukwuma's girlfriend. Chukwuma told him that Tina was his sister, without knowing that the man was already in love with Tina.

The man went to the British embassy in Dakar to apply for a visa for Tina. That day Chukwuma would have killed the white man for taking his girlfriend away from him, but the man ran back to his hotel.

Finally, Tina traveled to London with the white man, and as she left her apartment, she started weeping as memories of her pains and suffering in Dakar came flooding back. Her parents did not know what she was doing in Dakar, and she hoped to never go into prostitution again. She was so thrilled the day she left Senegal.

While she was in London, she kept sending money to Chukwuma to help him support himself in Senegal.

For many African ladies who were not lucky enough to find a white man to marry them and take them to Europe, the story is different. They had the alternative of sponsors. Sponsors paid money to get these African ladies to Europe (especially Italy), and once they got there, all they did was prostitution. They had to work and live with their "madam" in Italy until they paid the madam off before they could make their own living.

Alice also told me what the African guys did in Dakar. If they wanted to travel to Europe, they would become "pilots." A "pilot" is someone who goes to the seaport, takes the sailors off the ship, and brings them to the clubs to hook them up with the African ladies there.

These ladies would then take the sailors to their homes where they lived, and if they had African boyfriends, they would leave the house for them. They might stay with the sailor for the entire day if the sailor didn't have any work to do aboard his ship.

The next day, they would put the sailor in a taxi, and the taxi driver would take them to the seaport. Sometimes these sailors would fall in love with a lady, and would then bring them on board their ship, hide them in their cabin, and take them to Europe.

In the evening, Alice took me to the seaport and introduced me to the African pilots there. All these pilots were from different African countries: Cameroon, Côte d'Ivoire, Gambia, Ghana, Guinea-Bissau, Liberia, Nigeria, Senegal, and Sierra Leone. All of them became pilots so they could hide on ships that were going to Europe.

She also took me to a place they called Seaman's Bar. There I met many of the sailors who worked aboard ships. These African pilots also piloted tourists who were coming from cruise ships. They also piloted some of the international students who study in Senegal.

She told me I had to go inside the seaport in Dakar to look for sailors and bring them to Seaman's Bar. Then I would start making a little money—that was the only way I could get on board a ship.

I learned that Seaman's Bar was just a name made up by Africa's pilots. Thousands of sailors went there to drink and look for ladies. Senegalese ladies usually went there to dance at night, which was why they named the place "Seaman's Bar." Sailors from oil tankers liked to seek out where all the hot black ladies came to dance, and that was where all their money and time went.

I became a pilot, figuring that the sooner I joined them, the sooner I would travel out of Senegal.

As I said earlier, when you became a pilot, you would bring the sailors to the clubs, and sometimes you would also bring them to the ladies. For each day you took the sailor out, the sailor would pay you twenty US dollars. Sometimes you could get up to fifty dollars from them. The ladies also paid the pilot if they wanted to take the sailors away from Seaman's Bar.

Some of the sailors also came to Senegal with their contacts. They used some of these ladies to take drugs aboard their ships. The military guards at the port authority gate sometimes took money and allowed the ladies to go on board. Then the ladies would get the chance to travel on the ship to Europe.

Many oil tankers came to Dakar's seaport from all parts of the world. Most of the tanker ships that came there were cargo ships. There were three seaports in Dakar. The first one was for the cargo and the oil ships, and the second one was for the fishing boats. The third one was for cruise ships.

People from different races came to Dakar aboard these tanker ships, and the guys who did the piloting job would take them into the city to show them Dakar.

When a tanker ship arrived at Dakar, the African guys presented themselves as the agents of Seaman's Bar. They would show the sailors some nice photos of the beer bar, clubs, beautiful places, and ladies too.

In the evening, when the sailors ended the day's work aboard their ships, they took their showers, sprayed a bottle of delicate perfume on their bodies, and prepared themselves to meet the popular ladies in Dakar's open club.

The military at the gate allowed some of these ladies or the African pilots into the seaport, but they did it because they got tips from the guys every day.

I became enthusiastic about the whole thing. If that was the way to reach Europe, I would go for it. I went to my uncle to tell him what I was about to do—join the guys at the seaport. My uncle said that he knew about that business of piloting and wished he had thought of that the first time he came to Senegal. He would have been in Europe a long time ago.

While I was living with Alice, she taught me all I needed to know about the piloting job. She knew one of the high-ranking army officers, and she took me to her. They made a document for me: a free pass into the seaport when I was piloting the sailors.

With that paper, I could go into the seaport anytime I wanted without giving the armed officers at the gate a tip.

The best time to go into the seaport to take the sailors out of the ships was 6:30 p.m.

One evening at 5:45 p.m., I went into the seaport to see what the port looked like, and I went on a Philippine tanker ship. Once I was aboard, the first person I met was their chief engineer. I showed him some pictures I had with me and presented myself as an agent from Seaman's Bar.

The Filipino chief engineer told me he'd been in Dakar twice, but he couldn't find any Seaman's Bar anywhere. The other pilots were looking at me and were making fun of me because I was the new pilot in the field. They all knew how to talk with the sailors and convince them to go into the city.

I needed to convince the chief engineer to go with me that evening. I called Alice on my mobile phone, and I told her about the chief engineer. Alice looked like a Latino girl. She spoke with the chief engineer, and that evening, he went to the bar with me to see Alice.

All the African pilots who were waiting for their sailors to be ready were angry with me because the first time I came into the seaport, I went out with the chief engineer.

From morning to night, I worked hard in the seaport looking for a way to hide myself in the tanker ship. But before you could hide yourself in any ship to travel to Europe, you needed friends who worked on the ship. Sometimes the sailors would catch people who hid in their ship, and they would throw the person into the high sea.

The business of piloting in Dakar was dangerous at night. Some of the Senegalese guys were very crazy to deal with. When they saw us walking with the white guys at midnight, they always liked to attack us. These guys would take away all your money, and you needed to run because they were ready to kill.

We would leave the sailors there and run away; they rarely attacked the sailors, only the Africans. They were not happy that we came to Senegal and took over their seaport and started piloting the sailors instead of them.

My uncle disliked the fact that I was piloting, but he had no issue benefiting financially from my hard work. Hence, after I started the piloting job and was making a pretty penny from it, my uncle always borrowed money from me. He would never pay it back, and I hated to ask him about it. I didn't have the heart to say no when I had some money with me. One night at midnight, the wife of my uncle didn't let him sleep because they were behind with their rent. His wife had paid the money already, but she wanted it back from my uncle. Normally, in Africa, the men pay the rent, but my uncle's wife borrowed money from her company because my uncle couldn't pay the rent.

That night, my uncle woke me up, worried he couldn't provide for his family. He told me he wanted to run away from Dakar because he had spent almost half of his life in Senegal.

I asked him, "What about your family if you ran away?" He told me that the three kids his wife had were not his own children. My uncle told me he got married to his wife without knowing that she had her own kids, and they never talked about it because the kids were not living in Senegal.

After they got married, both of them were living alone for two years, but one day, his sister-in-law came in with some kids. She told my uncle's wife that she needed to take over her responsibilities. When he found out that his wife already had kids from another man, he was not happy about it.

Before he met his wife, he had some money with him to start up a business, and he didn't know that his wife's family liked him because of that. He said that it was very difficult for a Senegalese woman to marry a Nigerian man, but they could be your girlfriend.

I didn't know the reason a Nigerian man and Senegalese woman couldn't marry or live together for a long time. Later I learned of various stories of women in Senegal who allegedly killed their husbands by poisoning them in order to gain their husband's property. My uncle also told me that his wife refused to have a baby with him. He said that he had to learn how to love and live with her kids.

I told my uncle that every African man had the right to marry the woman of his choice in any part of the world without knowing her family's background.

But in the Nigerian culture, most men would never get married without his family knowing who the woman was. The first thing his family would do was get information about the woman and her family. If either family found anything that was wrong, the man and the woman wouldn't get married to each other.

But some men who were so in love with their ladies would run away to another city and get married there without either family knowing, and sometimes they didn't come back to see their parents again.

I was sad about what my uncle told me, so I went to his wife and asked her why she didn't want to have a baby with my uncle and told her that my grandmother, the mother of my uncle, was not happy that my uncle had no son or daughter of his own, and my uncle was the only son in their family.

She told me that my uncle didn't have a good job, and she didn't want her baby to suffer. That was the only reason. What little money I'd made since I started piloting at the Dakar seaport I gave to my uncle's wife. I now had to start saving money all over again, but my uncle still wanted to control me even while I was living with my girlfriend.

Every day from Monday to Sunday, I had to go to the seaport to look for a new ship that came that day. One evening, I was inside a taxi waiting for the two sailors who were with me, and I was singing praises to God for showing me the best way to leave the piloting business. The only reason I'd joined the piloting business was because that was the only way I could travel to Europe. Once I got to Europe, I would look for a better thing to do.

I was with the two sailors and two African pilot guys, and we were in the same taxi coming back from the club. In Senegal, some of the taxi drivers are villainous, mostly when you come from another African country.

The taxi driver saw we were with sailors, and that they were white guys, so he thought we had money with us. He made up an excuse that he needed to take a diversion while all he wanted was to take us to where the bad guys were. Everyone who lived in Dakar knew Kolobane Road, which was close to a gigantic market.

I told the taxi driver that I'd prefer to walk the rest of the way home, and I left with the two sailors. The other two African pilots who were with me knew Kolobane was a terrible place to walk on at night. Good taxi drivers would never drop you off there at night. The taxi driver dropped them off there, and the next day, I heard in the news that two guys were ambushed at night with knives.

Later that day, I found out that the two pilots were the ones who got attacked with knives. They cut the pilots like someone would cut an orange. I thanked God that they didn't die. My girlfriend, Alice, was kind enough to take care of them at the hospital.

One evening, I was leaving the seaport with four sailors, and we were looking for a taxi. I stopped a taxi without knowing that I had stopped the same taxi driver who took the two African guys to the bad guys. I went into his taxi with the sailors, and the taxi driver recognized me immediately.

He turned his head and looked at me. Then I realized that he was the same taxi driver. I told him to stop his car, that we wanted to get out. He became angry and asked me why. Then he locked all the doors of the taxi.

I told the taxi driver that we wanted to go back to the seaport, that the sailors forgot their passports. The taxi driver started speaking in the Senegalese language, Wolof. I understood a little; he said that I didn't know that he was a mafia taxi driver. The man put his hand under his chair and pulled out a big knife. He wanted to hit me with it—the taxi driver was driving with his left hand. He used his right hand to hold the knife.

I jumped from his taxi while he was still driving and rolled about on the road. He drove away with the four sailors who were with me. The next day, I went back to the seaport to see if the four sailors were on board; I was happy to see they were. They told me that the taxi man was crazy—that he took all their money and dropped them off at the club.

CHAPTER 11

Opportunity Missed

IN 1998, I ALMOST TRAVELED from Senegal on an oil tanker that came from Central America. One day, I went to the seaport, and I boarded an old ship that came from India. There I met an African pilot who told me he had heard another pilot saying that he was going to my house with the captain of the ship. The Central American ship had arrived at a different port, not the port where we were piloting. The seaport I was piloting was empty that day. All the ships had gone to Europe.

I went back to my house because of what the pilot told me about the American captain. When I got home, I saw Alice was in the house with the captain, a fifty-eight-year-old man.

I was angry to see that she was with him, but I couldn't say anything to her because that was a part of her job. I had no problem with her, since she had explained to me why she was doing that. She'd never gone after the black guys in Senegal since I had known her. She was only doing this business to save money to get out of Dakar. I didn't have any money to give her, so she had to go on living that crazy life of hers. Most of her friends in the same business also never wanted to do anything with guys from Dakar.

I thought that Alice would have called me on her phone and mentioned the man she had in our house. I never wanted her to hang around with guys I didn't know. She told me the same thing when we started our relationship. She never wanted me to do anything with the Senegalese ladies while I was in Dakar.

In the year 1997 when I met Alice, she was thirty-three years old, and I was twenty-eight years old. We understood each other, and we knew Dakar was a tough place to live in, yet she always tried to see that I got out of Senegal before she did.

Back to the captain with whom she was. His name was Mario, and he was born in Central America. He came to Dakar to refuel his tanker, and their ship stayed at the dock for a few days.

Alice introduced me to Mario because I once worked with one of the fishing boats that came from Spain. Alice also introduced me to the captain of that fishing boat, and I worked with them for a couple of months, but their contract in Dakar was too short. Their fishing boat only went to the Cape Verde Islands to fish. When they went back to Spain, I tried to go with them, but they refused because of the seaport authorities.

Mario spoke only Spanish. The man who piloted him came from a country in Africa called Sierra Leone. His name was Sony, and he didn't know that Alice was my girlfriend until the day he came with Mario to my apartment. If Sony knew I was living with Alice, he would never have brought Mario to our apartment that day.

Sony did not like me for a reason. Sometime ago, when I started piloting, he was one of the African pilots who were making fun of me because I didn't ask them to teach me how to pilot sailors around the city. Most of the African guys at that seaport were jealous and angry because they found out that Alice had taught me everything about piloting.

The day I saw Mario in my apartment, he was smoking, drinking, and dancing to Spanish music. Sony was sitting outside my apartment, drinking and smoking weed. Immediately when I entered the house, Mario became afraid and went outside because he thought Alice lived alone.

Alice told him I was her brother in front of Sony, and the pilot smiled because he knew that what Alice said was not true. The captain was not happy with the way I was holding Alice. He became jealous, and he had told her he wanted to marry her. He'd fallen in love with Alice, and he asked her why she came to Dakar to do this dirty business.

She told the captain that it was the only way she could raise money to leave Dakar with her brother. The captain felt so sad for us and promised to take us to his ship, which he told us was going to Central America.

The captain was a nice man, but the Sierra Leonean pilot betrayed us because he was the one who translated the language for us. Mario spoke only Spanish, and the Sierra Leonean pilot spoke Spanish too. He once lived in Spain for eight years before the Spanish immigration authorities deported him back to Africa.

Mario really wanted to help, and he asked Alice and me if we had our passports with us. The captain told Alice that she should not be worried, that once their ship got to Central America, he would propose marriage to her.

What I and Alice agreed on when we were living in Dakar was that we would take care of each other and be there for each other. But once we got to Europe, I would go my own way, and she would do the same, too, because we both knew that I did not mean for us to be together. We had different dreams about how our lives would be.

The captain said that the ship would stay in Dakar for only four days; he told Sony to go back to the city and that he was not coming back on board until the next day.

I was sitting on my couch all night long, and my prayer that night was for God to help me so I could hide myself in his ship and that the authorities should not catch me. I was totally tired of staying in Dakar. Senegal was not a place where you could work to survive.

The next day, the Sierra Leonean pilot came back to my house to check if everything was okay with the captain. It was a strange night. We didn't talk with the captain because we couldn't speak Spanish, and the man was making jokes. He got drunk, and he slept it off.

He told the pilot to go back to his ship and tell the chief officer and the chief engineer that he would not be on board for two days. It was difficult for me to get close to Alice because the captain was there, and he kept his eyes on me. The same day, the pilot returned to my apartment with the chief engineer and the chief officer.

When they saw Alice, they said it was no wonder the captain was falling in love. They all sat down and started smoking Marlboro cigarettes. They wanted to go back with the captain, but he refused to go with them.

From the day the captain came to my apartment, I didn't go to the seaport to check if there were any ships that came in. The captain slept in my apartment for three days and still refused to go back on board, though they had only four days to stay in Dakar.

On the third day, the pilot came to my house, and the captain was still with Alice. The pilot told Alice that he was not a foolish man at all. The pilot said that he went on board that morning and the sailors told him that the captain was planning to take Alice and her brother to Central America.

The pilot was furious, and he said that he came from Sierra Leone and wouldn't end up dead in Dakar—that he had already planned how to hide himself on that ship so he could travel to Central America.

Alice asked him if he had a Sierra Leonean passport with him, and he said no. She told him he needed his passport with him in case anything happened on the ship so that the authorities could easily identify him.

The pilot said that was not a problem. If he had money, he would have bought an African passport. He was using a Cameroonian passport, but he sold it because he needed money. He could buy another African passport from the Cameroonian guys, but he didn't have money for it.

Alice told the Sierra Leonean pilot she would do her best to get all of us on board, and they had one more day to stay in Dakar. Alice gave him 480 US dollars in front of me, and the pilot left. Within one hour, the pilot came back again. When I saw him, my spirit felt so cold. I knew that something was wrong. The pilot said once again that we were not leaving Dakar on the ship. He started calling the captain, who was sleeping. The pilot wanted to wake him up.

The Sierra Leonean pilot said to Alice, "You and your boyfriend cannot buy your way out of this."

Alice asked him, "What kind of twisted mind do you have?" He wanted to travel alone with the captain to avoid any interruptions from the seaport authorities. He was about to tell the captain that we were not related, that we were two lovers looking for a way to leave Dakar.

The noise that we were making woke the captain, and the envious pilot told the captain what was going on. Mario couldn't believe what the pilot told him. The captain later found out the truth, and he left Dakar with none of us on the ship.

The Sierra Leonean pilot was later caught by the police when he was traveling from Dakar to Gambia and deported out of Dakar.

CHAPTER 12

Desperation—My Exit Attempt at Bamako

EACH DAY THAT SHIPS ARRIVED at Dakar, all our conversations would be centered around how many people would hide aboard ships that week. We also knew the time every ship came to Dakar in the morning and at night. I always knew when a ship was about to arrive in the harbor because a member of the coast guard always passed the information to us.

Each day in Senegal, I knew how many people did or didn't make it out of Dakar aboard ships. I considered going to the next village, close to Morocco, where they said that it was easier to get to Europe. In Morocco, people paid money to cross the ocean on tiny boats, but it was very dangerous because they could only cross at midnight. If anything went wrong, everyone on the boat would die.

Thousands of African immigrants crossed the Atlantic Ocean to Spain each week, in search of a better life. I heard that the European Union opened an office in Bamako to help the Malians get back to Europe legally and also to assist those who had returned from Europe.

In October 1998, Alice and I went to Bamako because of the European Union office there. It had been a year since I left Bamako to go to Senegal, and I didn't know the city very well.

Thousands of Malians and other Africans were living illegally in France, and the French government sent many of them back to Mali and stopped any further arrivals to Europe by boat.

The Malian government was helping France deport Africans back to their countries. Almost every month a charter plane full of Malians and other Africans arrived in Bamako from Spain after being deported.

France was trying to get Mali to sign an agreement that would create an overall framework for dealing with immigrants in Europe. Many Africans went to Mali to see if they could travel to Europe with the help of the United Nations.

I went to Bamako with a UN ID card for over two weeks, hoping that I would get help traveling to and settling in Europe. They caught many people with the fake ID cards, and mine was among them.

As punishment, the authorities took us in a vehicle, deep into the desert—a long distance from the city—and abandoned us there. We wandered around for almost two months. The hot temperature in that desert was hell, and we suffered there before we could get back to Dakar again. There was no food, and the dust was so thick that you could hardly see or breathe. Some men with me could not urinate because they were so dehydrated. It was so bad that some guys would pay others for their urine so they could have some way of replenishing the fluid in their body. The only way I survived was because I had learned growing up in my mother's church how to fast and pray for days. I immediately fasted and did not need food or water once it ran out.

CHAPTER 13

Departure from Dakar— Perils of the Sea

WHEN I RETURNED TO DAKAR, I heard about a warship full of marines from France.

I was told they had arrived carrying up to five hundred military troops because of some politicians who were trying to fight the government of Senegal. The year I came to Dakar, the president of Senegal was Abdou Diouf, and his longtime opposition leader, Abdoulaye Wade, was fighting his government to get him to step down. We couldn't go to the seaport to pilot for a while because there were so many military troops.

In Dakar, many young people disliked Diouf's government. Wade and his allies rejoined the government as ministers of state in March 1995. He and the other ministers began preparing to democratically take over the government by March 1998.

We all thought that they would elect Wade for the National Assembly in February 1998 in the parliamentary election, but they didn't. So, he became upset and announced his resignation from the National Assembly in late July 1998, claiming Diouf's government was corrupt.

Almost all the Senegalese people supported Wade, and he later went to France, spent a year there, and returned to Senegal on October 27, 1999, and fought to win the parliamentary election again.

This was a problem for us. There was no movement for all the African pilots because of the elections. Every morning I used to go to the seaport with a friend of mine, and all we did was talk and plan how we could hide on a ship.

At 6:40 a.m., on March 19, 2000, while Alice and I were still sleeping, a friend of ours called me on my mobile phone saying that he had good information for me. He told me that a ship from Greece in the Dakar seaport boarded that day, and that there were many opportunities to travel with them.

He also said that in six hours, the ship would leave Dakar for an island in Spain, Tenerife. Two African pilots were planning to hide on that ship because they'd been piloting the sailors of that ship.

When he told me all this, I immediately took my mobile phone with some of the little money I had been saving for a long time, which was around 600 US dollars.

Alice was still sleeping, but I woke her and told her I was going to the seaport, and I would soon be back, without knowing that was the end of my stay in Dakar.

When I got to the seaport, the two pilots about whom my friend told me didn't want anyone to go on board with them. The moment they saw me, they became furious, and they told me that the ship belonged to them. They told the Senegalese security man who was guarding the ship not to allow me on board.

The two of them were not on board yet because the Dakar coast guard was checking the ship. I was not planning to take that ship out of Senegal that day.

The name of that oil tanker was *La Lisa,* and it came from Greece. The ship was full of a mixed crew. If you were planning to hide yourself on any oil tanker, you had to make sure that the ship was a mixed crew. A mixed crew was always good because they most likely wouldn't kill you or throw you into the sea if you were caught.

Alice had saved her own money. We were planning to buy an African passport to enter any European country, but that was a risk too because we could be deported back to Senegal. That day the Senegalese immigration was deporting people to Mali. Alice called me on my phone and asked if I was still at the seaport. She said that I needed to come back home. It was a Sunday, and every place was closed, though Immigration was still making its rounds.

The coast guard left, and the ship was about to move out of Dakar. But the coast guard was not very far away from the ship yet. The two African pilots watched the coast guard leaving the ship, and immediately they jumped on board *La Lisa.*

I was standing there, watching. They gave all the Senegalese money they had with them to the Senegalese security man, without knowing that the coast guard was not far away from the ship. When the coast guard noticed the movement of the guys jumping onto the ship, they turned their boat around and boarded the ship to search for them. After the four coast guards went on board, I didn't know what moved me to go after them.

The Senegalese security man tried to stop me. I tried to bribe him my mobile phone and the Senegalese money I had on me, but he refused all that I gave him.

Most of the time I lived in Nigeria and other African countries, I had never been in any position to do what I really wanted to do. But on March 19, 2000, I had a choice to make—to stay in Dakar or to take that ship.

I knew that for any choice that I made in my life, I would face the consequences—but if it went well, glory be to God. The Senegalese security man who was on duty that day knew that I was a pilot because every time I had to go aboard a ship to take a sailor out to the city, I had to pay him money before he would allow me to board the ship.

I pushed the security man away, ran inside the ship, and hid myself in the engine room.

Whatever you plan on doing in life, don't allow enemies of progress distract you. There were two attempts already to prevent me from boarding that ship. However, when God is the one leading you, no one can stop you.

The coast guard was still inside the ship searching for the two African guys. Where I hid was horrible and boiling hot. My face was burning, and my shoes were melting because of the heat from the engine room.

While I was still in the engine room, I saw that the two African guys had been picked up by the coast guard. One of the African pilots named Morgan saw me where I hid. He pointed at me so that the coast guards would see me, but when they looked in my direction, they did not see me. However, I could see them. So, they took the two pilots out of the seaport. It's still a mystery why and how they couldn't see me because we were so close, and I believe we even made eye contact.

I was so afraid to be caught by the coast guard. They delayed the ship for over three hours, and I was still in the engine room. My whole body was burning from the heat that was coming from the engine room. I became so exhausted and asked God to keep me alive so I could get to my destination.

I was praying in my mind and calling on God to allow the ship to leave Dakar. When we finally left, I said, "Amen." I hid myself on board at 2:31 p.m., and the ship left Dakar around 7:20 p.m. that same night.

When I saw the ship was moving away from Senegal, I came out of the engine room. I couldn't touch some parts of my face because it was so sore from the burning heat. I thanked God Almighty for the opportunity to hide myself on that ship.

Some people may not understand why we, African people, are killing ourselves just to get to Europe. Many Africans believe it is better to die trying to get to Europe than to suffer and die in Africa. Those who have tasted the hard life in Africa know what I am saying.

The ship left Dakar for Tenerife, Spain. However, I had another big problem on board the ship. I didn't come with any food or water because I left my house in Dakar very early in the morning to go to the seaport, not knowing I would be leaving Dakar that day.

Not one sailor aboard the ship knew there was a stowaway on board. I had been hiding for three days so far. I would hide in the morning in the engine room, and at midnight, I would come out on the deck and stay there to get some fresh air.

I later became weak and tired from not consuming any water or food. But the sailors made a mistake too because they left Dakar with no food on board. The Greek captain told the sailors that the company would send cartons of food for them when the ship got to Tenerife. Based on the condition of the ship, a journey from Dakar to Tenerife could take seven days to get there.

On the third night, one sailor saw me where I was hiding and asked me about the two other African pilots who had hidden on board the ship. I told him they didn't make it—that the coast guard took them off the ship. The sailor took me to an empty cabin, and when he was about to leave, I told him I was hungry. He said there was no food on board.

He later brought me one bottle of Spa water and cheese that already melted and told me that was the only thing they had on board. My stomach was empty for over four days. I gratefully drank the water and ate the cheese he gave me.

I was too tired, but I kept on forcing myself to drink the water and to eat the cheese. And I became so weak and couldn't stand up. I had to hold the door so I could stand.

When we'd been on the ocean for five days, around 3:15 a.m., all the lights in the ship suddenly went off, and the ship stopped moving because the engine was off. There was total silence on board.

Today I try not to think about what happened that night because I was so afraid and thought that my life was over. I will share it with you and pray that God would never allow such a night to repeat again.

The ship started shaking. I tried to stand up, but I couldn't because the shaking was too severe. If I had stood, I would've fallen again. Finally, I grabbed the door and opened it, but I restrained myself from going outside because the Greek captain didn't know that I was on board his ship.

Water was coming inside the tanker. All the doors were opening and closing, and all the glass cups, plates, and televisions had broken. The ship's shaking was worsening, and there was no noise or sign of the ship's sailors.

With no one controlling the ship, it was tossed up and down and swayed from side to side in the midst of a huge, scary storm. I thought I was all alone on the ship, which looked as if it was starting to sink. I thought I was in a nightmarish dream.

It looked like the ship had been abandoned for a very long time. There was no sign of anyone on board. Everywhere was in total darkness. I was told of the risk of going to Europe on a small boat but didn't realize that every ship, regardless of the size, could be affected by the weather. It thrilled me to travel to Europe on a ship, but not in that way. I thought that the smaller ships were more easily affected than the bigger ones.

People always talked about storms sinking ships, but that day I saw it with my own eyes. It terrified me to the point I thought I would die. I didn't know what to do or where to run to. I cried like a baby and gripped the door as though it could keep me from falling into the ocean.

My voice was very low from mostly not eating or drinking for five days. No one could hear the noise I was making. I cried out, "God Almighty, it looks like you do not love me anymore."

I made all kinds of promises to God to save my life and the ship. To my right, I saw a life jacket sliding from side to side and tried to reach for it. It was very difficult for me to pick it up because the ship was being tossed around so much.

When I finally reached the life jacket, I found a whistle on it. I put my hand out of the door and started blowing the whistle as hard as I could.

There was still no noise and no sign of the ship's sailors. The entire ship was totally dark, the engine was off, and the water was coming inside the whole place for over one and a half hours as the ship was tossed up and down.

It was my prayer, the promises I was making to God, and the whistle I blew that woke all of them up. I have this gift of feeling and sniffing out evil spirits when they're around me. While I was crying, praying, and blowing the whistle harder and louder, I felt that the spirit of death had taken over the entire ship. It appeared there was a conspiracy to maintain the silence so that the ship could go down into a watery grave.

I was asking God for his mercy and his miracles when I heard a sailor blowing on his own whistle. I was so relieved that I was not alone on the entire ship. While my head was outside the door, I heard the captain saying, "Start the engine," and all the sailors started running up and down.

That night was strange and chilling—one filled with fearsome adventures that are better heard than experienced. I kept this story within me for eighteen years with no one knowing about it, but the truth was that that night gave me a testimony to share—a testimony of God's greatness and mercies. To God be all the glory.

Finally, the captain could control the ship again, and the sailor who knew that I was on board came to my cabin and asked if everything was okay with me. I told him I could not understand what was going on—that not even one person came outside. He told me they didn't know what was going on, and that he woke up because of the noise of the whistle.

When he woke up, he saw their ship was shaking, water was everywhere, and it was totally dark. They had to use their flashlights to start the engine. The captain would have claimed that they were all drunk, but there was no drink or food on board. The little food they had was only canned food.

When the power came back, half of the ship had no lights, and the sailors started cleaning the entire ship from that night until morning the next day because so many things had broken.

Having drunk only water for seven days, I became exhausted, with no energy left in my body. When I tried to walk or stand up, I fell within a second. I had no energy to do anything. Our ship got to Tenerife in the evening of the seventh day. The weather was freezing. The ship did not, however, berth at the harbor.

Only one sailor knew I was on board—the one who helped keep me in a cabin. The same day that the ship reached Tenerife, the sailor came to my room to tell me they were going out to the city. I became frustrated because we were not in the harbor, and there was no way to get off the ship.

The coast guard came with a small boat to pick up some sailors who needed to go back to their country, and the sailor who put me in the cabin was among them. The sailor came with two life jackets and told me that one life jacket was for me—that I could swim to the land, because the ship didn't berth at the harbor.

Quite unfortunately, the ship happened to be miles away from the harbor. I said to myself, "God has brought me out here to abandon me, because I couldn't swim." This is a problem that most Africans have—the inability to swim. In Africa, our parents did not have the time to teach us how to swim. In Europe, while you're still a kid, your parents would take you out all the time, just to teach you how to swim. That's not the typical African mentality.

That day, half of the sailors left the ship for the airport because their contracts had expired. While they were on their way home, the new sailors came on board. Truly, it was a tough moment for me, as I was not prepared for such a situation.

That night, the weather on the ocean was freezing, and I already felt cold because my stomach was empty. Honestly, I didn't want to go back to Africa at that moment, and I did not want the authorities to catch me on board. If they caught me, they would send me back to Senegal.

It was frigid, and I couldn't stay much longer on board before the captain of the ship would discover me. I knew that in Dakar, that captain had been very aggressive to the sailors.

From the top of the ship, I could see the city of Tenerife very well. At night, you could see all the lights, but in the daytime, the clouds covered everything. I couldn't see the city anymore.

I waited patiently until it got dark. By that time, all the sailors were sleeping, and I heard that with a life jacket, you could swim. I encouraged myself, and I put the life jacket on my body and tied it very tight.

When you look from the back of the tanker ship down to the water, the distance is terribly far. That night, I found a rope on the deck, and I used it to climb down from the ship. The rope was too short, and my feet couldn't touch the body of the ship, so I jumped off the back of the tanker ship into the water.

When I was on top of the ship, I saw all the lights that were shining from the city. However, when I fell into the water, the entire island vanished.

I was so lucky that the propeller on the ship was not working because the engine was off. It would have crushed me to pieces. When I jumped into the water, I landed in front of the fan.

The weather and seas were rough, and I didn't know which direction to swim because I couldn't see the city lights again. I had never in my life swum for over three minutes, but that night, I was just too tired to move an inch.

The weather conditions were extremely cold with strong winds. My teeth were chattering, and I no longer was breathing well. The water had already taken me far from the ship, and it terrified me. I tried to get close to the ship, but the seas wouldn't let me.

Many African pilots with whom I worked at Dakar's seaport had gone to Europe with ships, but not one of them experienced what I went through.

My entire body started freezing. No one knew I was in the water, so no one could help me. Trying to swim to the city wasn't working. I started shouting and lost my voice from the cold temperature.

There was no one out there to hear except a couple of ships, but none of them could hear me because of the crashing of the sea waves. My voice was not strong too. I took the whistle out of the life jacket and started blowing on it, but it was not loud enough. I was too tired to blow it.

Even as I write this, I still experience vivid recollections of the desperation, the fear, and the anger. I never pray to pass through such an experience and the accompanying trauma again.

I couldn't swim back to the ship, and no one could hear me shouting for help. It totally pissed me off. I then remembered the name of the Lord, my God. I started crying and calling on him for help, though I could hardly verbalize my words because my teeth were chattering.

God had never failed me in the past, and I said, "You will not fail me now." Somehow the spirit of fear came over me, and I became troubled. I started taking off the life jacket so that I could sink down into the ocean. I had totally given up because I had no strength. No one could hear me, and probably no one cared. But I couldn't loosen the life jacket, though I kept trying to pull it from my body. The truth was that I simply didn't know what I was doing.

My eyes started closing, and I didn't know if I was falling asleep or if it was death approaching. All I could remember at that moment was that my whole life passed in front of my eyes like a movie.

I was not crying again, and I only heard the noise of the ocean and the noise from my chattering teeth. I was trying to open my eyes, but I couldn't. Then I started asking God for his help again.

There in the ocean, I made many promises to God. One promise was that my kids (whom I didn't have yet) and I would worship him forever if he would save me from the ocean.

I said these prayers in my mind, thanked him for everything, and confirmed once more that I never wanted to be separated from him, no matter how great the material desires may be. I wanted to be with him and my loved ones and asked Jesus Christ to come into me. I then said "Amen."

It was the worst experience of my life, and I screamed the more, though no sailor could hear me. I then put my head down.

That was the day I knew that God Almighty, the Alpha and the Omega, answers all prayers and also hears all you say, even when you think no one is listening. Almost before I finished praying, an enormous wind started blowing, and the water lifted me up and down, pushing me closer and closer to the ship.

God is great!

In the afternoon, when the sailors were leaving the ship for the airport and the coast guard came to pick them up, they used a rope ladder to get onto the boat of the coast guard. That wooden rope ladder was still outside, hanging on the side of the ship. The ladder was swinging to the left and to the right because the wind was blowing it around.

My hands couldn't grab the rope ladder, and the water kept tossing me up and down until another gigantic wave came and lifted me up, high enough that I could catch hold of the ladder. The distance between where I was in the water and the hanging rope was approximately six feet.

It was a miracle. I was holding my hand on the ladder, but I still couldn't lift my feet up to put them on the ladder because the lowest part of the ladder was about six feet from the water surface.

I kept holding the ladder with no energy and strength left in me, all my body still frozen. I hung on it for a couple of minutes, and I cried because I was too tired to continue hanging on.

While I was still holding the ladder, I started speaking to God. I said, "Please, God, I can't climb this rope ladder without you." I kept saying it, over five times in total.

Within a few seconds, the sea waves started tossing very hard and lifted me so high that I could put my feet on the rope ladder. When I saw I was standing on the wooden rope ladder, I was so tired that I closed my eyes for a few minutes.

When I felt I had gained a little strength, I started climbing up the ladder like a newborn baby.

CHAPTER 14

Apprehended!

I DON'T KNOW IF I would have lived to tell this story if the rope ladder was not hanging over the ship that midnight. I kept on climbing until I got on board. I couldn't stand on my feet and fell like a tree on the deck motionless. I did not at that point know if I was sleeping or if I had fainted.

I slept for a couple of hours, exposed to the terrible cold. While I was still lying on the floor of the deck, the sailors started the engine to warm the crude oil they had on board.

The crude oil became warm, and the deck became hot. I immediately started feeling warm. When I woke up, water was everywhere around me on the deck. It was water that came from my wet body and clothes. I felt like a thawed-out steak.

I wanted to hide myself again so I would not be seen lying on the deck, but I felt so exhausted that I couldn't easily stand up. I staggered as I walked along on the deck and fell again. My ankles hurt, and my hand seemed dislocated. I had injuries all over my body.

I stood up again and fell on my left shoulder. The pain was horrible, and it still hurts me to this day. If I knew I would have hurt myself so badly trying to walk, I would've remained where I was on the deck until the sailors saw me.

While trying to hide myself, I fell and hit my head on an iron bar. I lay there until the next morning, when a Russian sailor found me and called the ship's captain.

That morning, one of their company agents visited the ship, and he came on board with many cartons of food. The agent and the captain took me to the captain's office, and the agent had a video camera with him. He started recording what I was saying while the captain asked me questions.

I was so lucky that the ship was ready to leave Tenerife in a few hours. The captain became afraid because he didn't tell the authorities that I was on board. They came on board to see if everything was okay before the ship left, and they wouldn't have been happy with the captain if they found out that someone who was not a sailor was on board.

I started crying and begging the captain not to let the authorities know about me. The ship's agent asked me why I didn't want to go back to Africa and said that the authorities would not kill me—that they would only send me back to Dakar.

I told the agent that life was very difficult for me and my family. That was why I took that risk. While the agent was talking to me, my whole body was trembling. I saw the authorities getting close to the captain's office.

They were planning on handing me over to the Tenerife authorities. I was also not happy that they were recording me on a video camera.

The agent told the captain that the Spanish authorities would put him in jail if they found out that the ship came in with me on board because I was not a sailor. The captain told the sailors to put me in one of their cabins and that they should provide me with food and clothes.

The ship left that day. I didn't know their last destination. I was totally disappointed that I didn't make it to Spain. After a couple of days, I got news from the sailors that their ship was going to Curaçao, in the Netherlands Antilles. I ran into my cabin and started searching for Curaçao on the map but couldn't find it anywhere.

I went back to the sailors and asked them where in the world this Curaçao was, because I had never heard about it. The sailors told me that Curaçao was part of the Netherlands Antilles, and it was in the Caribbean.

I became worried because I had never in my whole life heard of a place called Curaçao, Netherlands Antilles. I felt so lost.

CHAPTER 15

"Promoted" to Ad Hoc Sailor

WHAT COULD I DO OR say that would stop the ship from going too far away from the El Dorado nations of my dreams? I spoke to the boss on board and asked how long it would take the ship to get to Curaçao, and the man told me it would take one month and two weeks to get there.

I went into my cabin and felt so frustrated. I started asking myself what kind of luck I had, to undergo so much pain and stress and not to get what I wanted in life. Europe was where all Africans loved to live. I didn't understand why fate was taking me farther and farther away from my dreams.

One thing I did not imagine before I started my journey was the possibility that God could have a unique plan for me.

The captain called me one early morning and told me he had a job for me, but that he wouldn't pay me. The reason he would not pay me is that I was a stowaway and had been eating, drinking, and walking about freely on his ship. I thus became an "ad hoc" sailor.

I started working with the boss man, Mario, on deck for one month and two weeks with no payment. The job I was doing was perilous. On the vessel, I helped with repairs, cleaned and removed loose rust, treated it with acid, and sprayed new paint over the surface. Sometimes a sailor would fall into the ocean while doing that kind of job.

My thoughts often drifted to Senegal. I knew that my uncle and Alice would be worried, because from Dakar to Spain was only seven days by ship, and they hadn't heard from me for over a month.

Day and night all my prayers were that God would make a way for me and give me strength and hope to go through this journey. Most nights I couldn't sleep. I often stayed awake crying, afraid of having to be made to go back to Africa after all the trials I had been through.

While I was on the ship, I found out that life on the high seas for a sailor consisted of eating, smoking, drinking lots of alcohol, and trying not to think about the days ahead—because anything could happen to a ship on the ocean.

On one occasion, I noticed a pair of shoes on the deck. Later that day, I found out that the owner of the shoes had jumped overboard. The sailor jumped overboard because of personal frustrations and the unhappy life he was living every day.

All the time I was aboard the ship, I never noticed him talking to anyone. Sometimes he came out to eat, and sometimes you would not even see him for days.

One sailor said that he was the victim's brother and couldn't believe he killed himself. The victim's brother said that his brother was not happy for over five years after he lost his family, and that it was the reason he became a sailor.

But he was really a vigorous man, never afraid to face hard situations. His mysterious death made me sad. It is always sad news when someone who is so young dies—when they take their own lives without thinking about how loved ones left behind will feel.

CHAPTER 16

The Ghosts of *La Lisa*—1

IT SURPRISED ALL THE SAILORS that I survived when I jumped overboard. They told me that most people who fell from the top deck into the sea do not survive it. They were not alone in their surprise. I did not know the reason I had survived all the perilous situations I passed through.

While I was talking with the sailors, some of them told me their stories, and why they became sailors. Most of them had experienced something in life that they couldn't handle, so they became sailors just for the opportunity to live a solitary life on the sea.

There was one mysterious phenomenon about our ship—*La Lisa*. I thought I was the only one who noticed it. If you came outside, you would seem to hear the sound of little children playing on the deck. Sometimes it would seem they were crying.

The ship scared the hell out of me. I didn't sleep at night because of the noises I heard. Sometimes when you opened the door to investigate, you would see a shadow pass by quickly.

Some sailors who noticed the same thing told me that the ship was a ghost ship, that they would hear the voices of people talking on the deck but wouldn't see them when they checked.

One day, when I worked much longer than usual on the deck, I became very exhausted. I really wanted to sleep, but I was afraid of the room where I was because a sailor had passed away there.

That night I thought of how long I would have to stay aboard the ship before I could get off. As I lay in bed thinking, I fell asleep and forgot all about the ghosts of *La Lisa*.

CHAPTER 17

The Ghosts of *La Lisa*—2

SOMEONE HIT MY HEAD, HARD. It was so painful that I cried, and wished it was a dream, but it wasn't. I believed that there were spirits living on the ship, because I believed they had tried to sink the ship before. I cried and held my head in my hands—the pain was too much. I was scared to tell the sailors what happened to me because a few of them had already encountered terrible things aboard the ship.

Some of them drank too much beer, or they took drugs so they wouldn't feel anything that happened at night. Life on the ocean was freezingly cold, and then there was the silence. Most times everywhere was quiet as a graveyard. Even the sailors did not talk much to each other. You could only communicate with a person who was from the same country as you.

Everyone on board kept much to himself—even the captain. The only time you could see sailors come together was when they wanted to eat food.

The ocean was beautiful, full of different colors of water, but when you observed the vastness of it, you would be intimidated and become scared.

I experienced many things while I was aboard *La Lisa*, and I pray to never again travel long distance by ship. If by some happenstance I find myself aboard a ship again, then it hopefully would not be for anything more than a five-minute journey.

CHAPTER 18

Land Ho!

I USED TO LOVE SHIPS and always liked to go aboard a ship when I could, but not anymore. After a long, frustrating month and two weeks on the ocean, we finally approached Curaçao, Netherlands Antilles.

I was on the top deck trying to see what Curaçao looked like because we arrived at night. A sailor came to me to tell me that the captain wanted to see me in his office.

It was a surprise to me that the captain had already informed the Curaçao authorities that I was on the ship. If I'd known that he had already informed the authorities that I was on board his ship, I would have long jumped from the ship and run away. I wished I could swim. Everything would have been easier for me if only I could swim.

The captain told me they were going to keep me somewhere where the authorities could see me. He said if the Curaçao authorities saw me moving around the ship, they would take him and put him in jail.

If the police took him, they would seize the ship, and the company would pay a lot of money to the Curaçao authorities. He told me I shouldn't be worried, that I wouldn't be long where he wanted to put me—I never knew that they had a prison cell on their ship.

Before the captain put me inside the prison cell, he told me to be strong. When I entered the prison cell of the ship, I felt as though all my dreams and plans for the good life had been caged—without the hope of actualization ever again.

CHAPTER 19

Curaçao, Netherlands Antilles

THE SHIP CAME INTO CURAÇAO, Netherlands Antilles, on the night of July 14, 2000, and July 14 was my birthday. I couldn't see the city clearly, and everywhere was dark.

In the morning, when I woke up from my sleep, I looked out from the window of the prison cell and almost had a heart attack at what I saw. I thought I was back in one of the African countries.

All the people living in Curaçao are black people. I had hoped that the people looked like the Europeans. The way everything was going with me, it was possible it could be God's plan for me to come to Curaçao. What more could I say? It certainly was not my plan, desire, or ambition.

That morning, two police officers came on board to see me. They came inside the prison cell and sat down with me. They asked me my name, where I came from, why I took the ship, how long I had been on the ship, and from where I got aboard the ship before coming to Curaçao.

I answered all their questions, and they told me they would not allow me on their island. The police officers said that they don't give political asylum here in Curaçao because I told them I needed political asylum.

They told me I had to go back with the ship to Africa, where I was coming from, and that they were sorry that they couldn't help me.

My dreams were over. I felt so sad, especially after the long, tedious, and horrible journey I had undertaken so far. The two police guys left the ship and told me to try again—that next time I might succeed.

CHAPTER 20

Hostage at the *La Lisa* Iron Prison Cell

THEY LOCKED ME BACK IN that room, and the ship had to stay in Curaçao for four days. From there, it would go back to Guinea-Bissau, an African country.

After two days of being locked up on board, I couldn't stand it any longer. I asked some sailors to help me so I could escape. All the sailors were afraid of the Curaçao authorities. The police had already cautioned them. I commenced my plans on how to escape from the ship. I had only two days left before it would set sail for Africa.

The room was tiny, and there was no place to break out through. The ship's prison cell was built all around with iron. I tried using my spoon to cut the iron from the window, but I couldn't.

My arms and my shoulder were hurting badly because I was trying to force the iron window open with my hands. My mind was many miles away. I would still be in the cell by tomorrow because there was simply no way of breaking out from that fortress.

I didn't have plans anymore. I felt so cold in my heart, so alone. I thought about all the things I encountered on my way to Tenerife Island in Spain, and about the miserable one month and two weeks spent to get to Curaçao, and now the authorities were planning to take me back to Africa.

I woke my spirit up and encouraged myself. I prayed and asked God for his help with what I was about to do.

CHAPTER 21

Escape from the *La Lisa* Iron Prison

IT WAS VERY EARLY IN the morning, around 7:00 a.m. I called for the chief cook to tell him I was hungry. The chief cook was a Filipino. He sent a sailor to bring me food in the room where I was locked up.

When the sailor opened the door, I told him I wanted to speak with the captain. That was the last day the ship would stay in Curaçao.

The sailor refused; he told me that the captain was busy signing some papers so the ship could leave Curaçao that night. The sailor was still holding the plate of the food with his hand, and he used his feet to hold the door.

Honestly, the sailor didn't know the predicament I was going through. At that moment, my whole life was upside down. I felt so depressed, worried, and frustrated. It was like I was facing a life-and-death situation. To go with the ship to Africa meant my aspiration was being taken backward, not forward, and the mindset of sojourners from Africa was forward ever—backward never. I would therefore go forward toward my dreams or die trying.

I pushed the food out of his hand, and while he was trying to catch the plate, he took his feet out of the door. The door was wide open. I jumped out and ran.

The moment I jumped out of the room, the sailor started shouting, "Captain, stowaway, stowaway!"

The prison cell where they kept me was located very high on the top of the ship's deck. I had to jump from deck to deck before I could make it to land. I was desperate and not thinking. I could have broken my neck, or worse. This was my last chance to escape before the ship set sail with me back to Africa.

When I made it to the ground, it was a big problem for me to run. I felt dizzy because of the impact of the dangerous high jumps I made. The sailors tried to chase me but couldn't dare to take the risk to jump off the high decks, so they used the steps to come after me.

CHAPTER 22

Hide-and-Seek at the Seaport Harbor

IN THE HARBOR, I COULDN'T find a place to hide myself. There was water everywhere because the harbor was a refinery. The captain informed the Curaçao authorities that I had escaped, and they started looking for me with their dogs.

Every place was wide open. There was no place to hide, so I forced myself under a small bridge, about nine inches high from the ground. I had to face my body up, my head to the side. I couldn't turn around to the left or to the right.

While the authorities were looking for me, they came and stood very close to me with their dogs. The dogs saw me—they looked at me as I looked back at them from under the bridge—but they didn't bark at me. The authorities couldn't find me because all the while I was under the bridge looking at their feet. I kept calling to God in my heart—asking for his mercies and protection. The mercies and providence of God indeed spoke for me in my moment of desperation.

The authorities searched for me for the entire day. I crawled out from under the bridge where I was hiding at 6:30 a.m. on Monday.

The day was not bright yet, and I set my mind on going from there into the city.

When I got to the gate of the refinery, I found it difficult to go through it. I went up and down without knowing what to do until all the people who were working in the refinery started coming in. When I saw many workers coming inside, I tried to communicate with them in English, but they didn't respond.

Everyone in the refinery was wearing a uniform. I was the only person who looked different from them. While I was walking around, I saw an overall uniform and yellow helmet hanging on the wall, so I took them and put them on. I looked like one of them now.

The language spoken in Curaçao is not English. Only a few of the educated people speak English. The official language on the Caribbean islands of Aruba, Bonaire, and Curaçao is Papiamento. The language is a mixture of Spanish, Portuguese, Dutch, English, and French.

I kept on walking around without knowing where to go. One worker who was passing by in his Toyota pickup saw me in their uniform, and he stopped his truck and asked me where I was going. He thought I was one of their workers because I was wearing their refinery clothes.

I couldn't respond to what he was asking me. I didn't understand the language he was speaking at that moment. The man tried to figure out why I was not talking to him, and he asked if everything was okay with me. I played like I was deaf.

When he asked me if I needed a lift, I answered yes with my head. He gave me a lift to the gate. While we were on our way, he started asking me more questions. I kept on acting like a deaf man, and he became tired of the signs I was showing him.

He stopped me at the gate, but the security was too tight. I didn't know what more to do. I had been walking around for the entire day and was totally exhausted. My whole body was in pain from jumping out of the ship. I was tired and ready to give up.

So, I went to the authorities at the gate and told them I was the one they were looking for who jumped out from the ship that came from Africa. All the officers became shocked, and some of them pulled out their guns. They asked me why I was wearing their refinery uniform.

I went to the authorities under the notion that the ship had already left the island of Curaçao. The authorities at the gate asked me the name of my country, and when I told them about Nigeria, they didn't believe me.

They told me I was not a Nigerian because their police had caught a couple of Nigerian people at the airport with different passports. Nigerians don't want to admit that they are from Nigeria. They always refuse to admit that they are from Nigeria because it is seen in an unpleasant light, and they are afraid to be deported back to Africa. I was aware that thousands of Nigerians always denied being Nigerian citizens when the authorities caught them in Europe without their documents.

I told the authorities that I didn't have my passport there to prove it, but truly, I was a Nigerian citizen, and I didn't want to go back to Africa.

My whole body was shaking while I was talking to them. The officer took me into the toilet and told me to sit there. It is not a straightforward thing when you have to face the authorities. I lost hope, but I kept on praying until the security officers heard the noise of my prayer.

God has his own plans, and in his own time, he makes all things beautiful and perfect. Immediately the manifestations of God started working around me. I didn't know that God Almighty already had plans for me, and his timing is always the best.

One of the police officers at the gate came into the toilet and told me that he heard what I was praying. He asked me if I was a Christian, and I told him yes.

The officer told me not to be worried, that he was a black man like myself, and that even if I came from another country, we were all children of God.

The man told me he would try to help me out of this mess because he could see I was not myself again. He called the two police officers who came on board when our ship arrived in the harbor of Curaçao. When the two came to pick me up, it was already evening. They put me in their police car and drove away. While we were on our way to their office, they stopped on a bridge called Queen Juliana. They were talking to each other in their language. I became afraid.

I didn't understand what they were talking about. I thought they were about to throw me over the bridge. One of them asked me where I hid when I jumped off from the ship into their harbor.

His partner then said to him that he should not ask me that kind of question for now. He also told him they should look for a way to help me out, but he still wanted to know where I had been hiding that made them unable to find me for one and a half days.

They exhausted me by their questions, which I was answering obediently. I told the two officers that I didn't want to go into detail about what happened to me or where I hid myself during the first day. His partner then reminded him of the saying to "never ask a navy man if he'd have another drink, because it was nobody's business how much he already had."

While we were still on the bridge inside the police car, they told me what they were about to do. They saw that my hands and my body were shaking. They then started their car and drove to the office but kept on saying, "We will not deport you."

They asked me why my body was shaking. I told them I was too tired from running and added, "Please, I need freedom. I don't want to be sent back to Africa."

On the way to their office, they resumed speaking in their language, Papiamento, and started making a couple of phone calls too. All I could understand while they were talking on the phone were the words "freedom, freedom," because they were using it to end their conversation.

CHAPTER 23

Miracle in Curaçao

WHEN THEY FINISHED MAKING THE calls, they told me that they were speaking with one of the good lawyers they had in Curaçao, and that he was going to help me.

These two guys were police officers. In fact, they were more than police officers—God was using them as his instruments. They told me they were going to help me stay in Curaçao. Before they dropped me, we spent an hour driving around the city. They then bought food for me and told me to be strong.

I thought that the ship had already left Curaçao. I never knew that the authorities told the captain that the ship was not going to leave Curaçao without me. For two and a half days, the ship had been in the harbor waiting for me.

I spent a night in one of the police stations in the city without knowing that the two police officers knew my ship was waiting for me. The next morning, they came to pick me up in a police car.

They took me to an office at the harbor. When we arrived, I saw that the ship was still there. The sailors were yelling at me, and saying, "Bring him on board." They were so frustrated and just wanted their ship to set sail.

I looked at the police officers, and they said again, "Just be strong." It was freezing cold in the room where I was kept. They handcuffed me and shackled my feet too.

The cold was so bad that I started hitting my body against the door. One of the police guys came and told me that their boss was in the office. They told me that the chief of police had already called the special police to put me back on board the ship, but that they were doing their best to keep me here in Curaçao.

While we were still talking, the five special police officers arrived and came into the room where I was. The two police officers started making more calls, and they told their chief that I had a lawyer.

The chief of seaport police asked them what that had to do with their job, and how it was that I had a lawyer while in their custody. The police officers then told their boss that the lawyer was on the line and wanted to speak with him. He ignored the call and ordered the special police guys to put me back on board.

All I could say was "Please, sir, do not put me back on board. I will die there." One of the special police officers he called to put me on the ship began pushing me out of the room where I was kept.

He then started giving me some advice, saying that I had to go back on board. He said that he was not the one who wanted me to leave Curaçao—that Immigration told him to put me back on the ship immediately.

I told him if he really wanted me back aboard the ship, then he had to kill me first because I was not going back aboard. They did not understand all the things I had encountered on the high seas that scared me so much. I was not ready to go back on the ship because I believed it was a ghost ship.

The chief of seaport police refused to understand the hell I went through. Of course, it wasn't his problem that I was in the predicament I was in.

I also told him that if he deported me back to Dakar, that meant that I would go back to the life I was once living that I had forsaken.

He told me that, unfortunately, they didn't have a time machine that could change my situation here in Curaçao—that he was sorry but wouldn't be able to help me with my request.

The lawyer called back again, but their chief still refused to answer the call. I looked out through the door, and I saw the authorities were coming with their small boat to pick me up. The ship was ready and was slowly moving away from the harbor. The authorities wanted to put me on their own boat and bring me to the ship.

I remembered the wooden rope ladder that I had so longed to reach when I was dying in the waters of Spain. This time I loathed the wooden rope ladder and was repulsed by the idea of climbing it to go aboard any ship. I was a mess that day and refused to go with the authorities. I had been in pain since the ship *La Lisa* came to Curaçao. I felt so miserable.

The moment I saw the ship standing in front of me, I felt a chilling sensation I will never forget. It gave me terrible memories and scared the hell out of me. I became so anxious and felt so sick that I started crying, and I threw up.

God really used the two police officers. They were not happy with the entire situation that was going on at their office at that moment. The two of them kept on calling the lawyer, and thank God, their calls paid off. The lawyer knew the governor of Curaçao, and the governor put a call through to the chief of seaport police—the one who wanted to send me away.

He didn't want to take any calls at all, and so the police officers told him, "Sir, we think you have to pick up this call." When he picked up the phone, the governor told him she was interested in my case and that she should keep me and let the ship go.

When I got the news, I felt an incredible gratitude to God, and colossal relief that I would now have time to stay on the island Curaçao. All my life I have known that there were good people who would help you according to the grace of God, and these two police officers were nothing short of godsend. After the call, the chief of seaport police became very angry with the two police officers and told them they should never try to tell him how to run his office.

They kept me in one of the empty rooms in their office. I was so exhausted by the whole episode and fell asleep almost immediately with the handcuffs still on my hands.

The whole thing happened in the morning around 10:00 a.m. I slept and woke up around 4:15 p.m. The chief of seaport police later came to me the same day and started asking me some questions.

I would have answered all the questions if I knew them all. He asked me in which month I was born. I told him July 14, and that our ship came into Curaçao, Netherlands Antilles, on July 14, 2000.

The chief shook his head and asked me again, "Who are you that everyone in my office was fighting for you to stay in Curaçao?"

He told me that even the governor of Curaçao called him on his office phone just to let me stay in Curaçao.

He also said he had never spoken to their governor before, and that my case had garnered much attention. He told me that he had been the chief of the seaport at the Curaçao harbor for many years, but he was shocked at what he saw that day, especially that some of his officers were trying to help me stay on their island. He said that he had never witnessed that before.

He also told me he had deported many illegal aliens who came into Curaçao by ship or boat, and no one had ever interrupted him when he was doing his job before.

But my case surprised him in that many people came to rescue me. He told me that I must be one of those with a special blessing from God who always got help in their life, and that this was what many people want to achieve in life—the freedom to live wherever they want. He said that the most important thing was that they would not deport me back to Africa. The governor had told him I could stay.

He called the two seaport security officers who helped me. He said to me that these two officers would take me to a place where I would stay in the meantime, and he wished me the best in Curaçao.

The two seaport security officers took me to a place called the "Foreigners' Barracks." The Foreigners' Barracks was a facility that the government of Curaçao had for the undocumented people to stay in until they deported them back to their countries. The facility was at the backyard of the Curaçao prison known as Bon Futuro Prison.

When prisoners finished their sentence, the authorities in the prison would send them to the Foreigners' Barracks, if they were foreigners. The prisoners would stay there until Immigration bought their ticket to send them away to their country. Some prisoners who were there were murderers. So, I asked the two police officers if there was any place else to keep me than this kind of place. One of them told me that the government of Curaçao had no place to put people in my situation, and that I would have to stay there for a while. They told me that a lawyer would get in touch with me, and they left.

CHAPTER 24

Life in the Foreigners' Barracks

AFTER THREE WEEKS, I PUT a call through to Dakar and got Alice on the phone. She couldn't believe her ears—that I was the one calling. I told Alice my entire story and where I was, and I spoke to my uncle too. They were happy to hear from me. I, however, wasn't able to reach my parents in Nigeria by phone.

Before the two police officers left, they told me that within two months, the lawyer would get me on the streets. The government would give me a place to stay in the city. The Foreigners' Barracks was full of Latino people. Many Latinos were living in Curaçao illegally.

The government built the Foreigners' Barracks with no windows. They used iron rods to fabricate the windows. It looked like a cage.

Inside the Foreigners' Barracks, there were only ten beds, but it was full of many people, with many of them lying on the floor. The two police guys surprised me. They came back to the barracks again in the morning with a bag full of new clothes.

They told me that one of the human rights organizations heard about my situation, and they gave them many things to bring to me. Most of the illegal people who were staying in the Foreigners' Barracks had nothing to wear, and they asked me why the police was doing all this shopping for me. I had to share all the clothes with them because some of them had stayed there for two or three months waiting for the government to buy their tickets.

I was happy that I was in Curaçao but was not happy to be locked up like a criminal. The security guards sometimes sent the prisoners from Bon Futuro Prison to come into the rooms where we were staying and clean the whole place. Whenever this happened, we were usually scared because some of them had committed dangerous crimes.

One day, a prisoner came inside to clean the room I was staying in. The boy was just nineteen years old. I asked him why he was in jail, and he told me that he killed one of his friends with a wooden stick. He was still happy that he killed his friend.

Another day, I looked out of the window and saw a prisoner being released from prison. He was jumping up and down because he was free. However, the same day he left jail, I learned that he robbed a place. He was caught, and within one or two days, he was back in the prison.

CHAPTER 25

Back and Forth with Curaçao Immigration

I THOUGHT THAT IN ONE or two months I would be out of the Foreigners' Barracks just as the two seaport security officers had told me. This was, however, not the case. There was no freedom at the barracks. I was just living there very much like a prisoner.

There was a small office inside the Foreigners' Barracks' yard. Security police officers stayed there to watch us so that no one would escape from the barracks.

Police at the Foreigners' Barracks were different from the police who protected the island of Curaçao. The Curaçao island police are called the Dutch Caribbean police (KORPS or KPCN), and they were the law enforcement agency of the Caribbean Netherlands. They maintained public order and operated under the authority of the island governor. The Dutch government was still responsible for the defense and foreign affairs of Curaçao.

The police who guard the barracks are known as the SKS—Servisio di Kòntròl i Siguridat (Inspection and Security Service). They're the local police. These officers opened the Foreigners' Barracks doors once a week so we could go into the yard to walk around the compound for just thirty minutes. They would then put us back inside the cells and lock the doors, and we would stay inside for another week before they'd open the door again. This was the regular routine.

Some of the SKS officers were quite nice to us. If the good ones were on duty, they would open the door for us twice a week to come outside for fresh air.

When I had stayed one month inside the Foreigners' Barracks, a lawyer came to look for me. He told me that the government had sent him to represent me. I was thrilled that a lawyer had finally been sent to me. The lawyer took down my entire story and said he would file a case so I could be out of the barracks within two months.

Life in the Foreigners' Barracks was horrible. The food was also awful. We were drinking from the same area where the toilet was, and there was no fresh air coming into the place. The toilet was filthy, and everything there was totally terrible. Even the prisoners who had committed crimes were living better than us.

Two months passed, and I heard nothing from my lawyer. I became really worried. I do not remember ever having a pleasant dream while I was inside the barracks. Every day, immigration officers would bring people they had picked up from the streets and put them in the same place with us.

Sometimes I would make a new friend there, and some of them would stay for two or three weeks. Oftentimes, before I woke from my sleep, they were gone.

One day my lawyer returned, and I told him I was getting mad inside this place. He responded that he was working hard on my case. He asked me if I had any identification with me—that he needed my documents to prove to the court that I was a Nigerian.

I told him I didn't have my documents with me, but I could ask my uncle who lived in Senegal to send them to me. The lawyer gave me his address and told me that when he got my Nigerian passport, everything would be easier.

The security guard in the Foreigners' Barracks allowed us to make a phone call once a week, and they would only allow five people to make a call per week. To make a call, they had to take us inside an office in the jail.

If any of us from the barracks had problems with a security guard that week, they would not allow any of us to make a call. Sometimes, as punishment, they made it difficult for us to use the toilet or shower. We'd have to wait the entire day before the guard would give us tissue paper and soap.

I waited for two weeks before the security guards gave me a chance to call my uncle in Senegal to ask him to send my passport that I kept in his house. My uncle sent my passport to the lawyer's address, but I heard nothing from the lawyer.

I kept on waiting. I called his office several times, but no one picked up the phone. Before I knew it, four months had passed. I couldn't reach the two police officers who helped me on the phone. At times, I would be all alone in that place, especially when the immigration officers would come in with tickets for everyone and send them away. The only time undocumented people could leave the Foreigners' Barracks quickly was if they could afford the money to buy their own ticket.

Five months had passed, and I still hadn't heard from my lawyer. I became more worried and disappointed. I felt I had been completely abandoned there. One day, immigration officers brought in many Jamaicans and Dominican people, filling up the Foreigners' Barracks. I was the only one who had stayed there five months continuously.

I walked up to the immigration officers and asked them about my lawyer. They told me they had nothing to do with my case, and that my lawyer had abandoned me there.

One of them told me that my lawyer went away for his honeymoon. He'd just gotten married, and he showed me the newspaper with the lawyer on the front page. The immigration officers told me I came to Curaçao to enjoy life, but that it was not going to be so easy. They said that my case would not be touched until the lawyer came back from his honeymoon, and that I was going to be staying a very long time in the Foreigners' Barracks.

I was dumbfounded at their insensitivity and didn't know what to say to them. All the people in the barracks, including the security guards, called me "Africa." They never called me by my name. "Africa" became my name. Even the immigration officers called me "Africa." I never disliked the nickname they called me—actually, it made me feel so special while I was inside there. They were all interested in knowing more about Africa. Some said they knew their ancestors came from Africa, and that they hoped someday they would be able to visit the motherland.

Sometimes the overall chief of immigration/police (not the chief of seaport police) would visit the Foreigners' Barracks because he was the one in charge. One day, I went to him to ask about my case. He never liked to answer my questions, and always told me he was waiting for my ship to come back to Curaçao, and that then, he would put me back aboard the ship. He told me he was the one who controlled Immigration and that his mind regarding my matter was, in his own words, "You should just be sent back to Africa."

After that day, Immigration started sending some papers to me, asking me to sign them. I refused to sign the papers because everything written on the papers was in the Dutch language, which I did not understand.

They told me that if I refused to sign it, I would be staying for a long time in Foreigners' Barracks. I then took the papers to one of the security guards to read them to me because Immigration refused to read them to me.

The security guard then explained to me what was on the paper. It stated that I was in Curaçao illegally, and that if the government sent me away, I wouldn't return to Curaçao for the next three years. That was what the Immigration gave to everyone they put into Foreigners' Barracks.

Immigration had said that signing the document was the only way they could look into my case. I was afraid that one day they would bundle me back to Africa as they had been threatening to do so for so long.

I always refused to sign the papers anytime they gave them to me. Every day that Immigration came and took some of the undocumented people and deported them, I became more afraid that it would soon come to the day that they would deport me out of Curaçao.

Not seeing my lawyer or hearing from him made me really worried. I had a lot to lose if I went back to Africa. I did not know what to do next. I felt totally lost and confused.

One day I called the Immigration and asked them to visit me—that I would tell them everything about myself. Four immigration officers came later that day and said to me, "Yes, we're working on your case to send you back to Africa. Why did you call us?"

I then changed my story just to remain in Curaçao. I told Immigration that I was not born in Africa and that my name was not Jerry Anyaene.

They were shocked and asked me why I was changing my story after they had arranged some documents to send me away.

I told them I just wanted freedom! I said, "If you send me to any African country without my passport, I will tell that country that I am not an African, and I will be sent back to you here in Curaçao." I promised them I would deny my identity in any country that they were planning to send me to because I didn't have my passport, and that in Nigeria, they did not register all the passports in their system.

They looked at each other, told me to calm down, and then said, "Since you have changed your story, you should tell us your name and the country where you were born so we can send you there."

I then told Immigration that I was born in America, in the city of Boston, Massachusetts.

CHAPTER 26

Riot at the Foreigners' Barracks

HONESTLY SPEAKING, I DID NOT know what I was doing. I don't even know how America came into my mind. I was confused at that moment. But they wrote down everything I told them. Immigration told me they would contact the American embassy in Venezuela to ask them if I was born in Boston. They told me that the information I gave them would be difficult to work on without my passport.

They left, but still my mind was not at peace. I was still afraid that they might change their minds and send me to Africa. At that moment, everyone inside Foreigners' Barracks started giving me advice about what to do and what to say. I felt so frustrated, and so I took all their advice.

The next day, Immigration came to get some undocumented people. I went to them and said, "Sir, I was not born in America, and my name is not Jerry Anyaene."

Immigration told me they were not here to play with me, that I should tell them where I was born. I replied that after I spoke with my lawyer, I would tell them everything they wanted to know about me. I didn't know that my lawyer worked with the government and couldn't keep my information safe. I thought that he was an independent lawyer. There is a lot that immigration officers know.

Still, they couldn't deport me. They had to wait for the lawyer to come back from his honeymoon. I was treated so badly inside the Foreigners' Barracks at a point that somehow, the thought of going back to Africa crept into my mind. Thankfully, everyone in the barracks who heard this idea was totally against it.

One day, some of the Jamaicans who were staying inside the Foreigners' Barracks with us started shouting and threatening that they would break out from the "illegal" barracks because they were tired of it. This was after only two weeks of stay there.

One of the SKS officers came to the window and told them to stop the noise, but the Jamaican guys refused to listen to the officers. The SKS officer called for backup from his group, and he made the call from his cell phone. I was sitting by the window, and he told me I should tell those illegal guys to close their mouths.

The Jamaican guys heard what the man said. They became angrier and made more noise. The SKS officer opened the door and told all of us to get inside a small cage. The cage was specifically made for people who tried to escape. They then locked us inside the cage with their keys.

There were six small rooms built like cages inside the cells in the Foreigners' Barracks. They looked like mini jail cells, with only a little space for us to walk around. Every room had its own iron gate. Throughout the over five months that I had been inside the barracks, the security officers had never locked those gates.

The main building had only one door leading inside. They always locked it with keys, so that there was no need to lock us inside the cage again. The main building already had security officers who were watching us every minute of the day.

That day I refused to go into the cage. I told them that I was locked up already. They all knew that I was not a troublemaker. I had been there for a very long time, and I'd never for one day disturbed or disrespected the officers who worked there.

I told the officers that the guys who were making the noise came in just two weeks ago and that they should talk to them.

Eight of the SKS police officers tried to pull me out of the window where I was sitting, and they asked me what gave me the boldness to talk to them.

I held on to the window, and they couldn't pull me from the window, so they started beating me. All eight of them kicked me with their boots. Some of them kicked my head. While they were kicking me, they tore off the clothes I was wearing.

When the SKS officers were beating me, one of them said, "This isn't Africa. You can't tell us what to do in our Foreigners' Barracks."

The SKS officers beat the hell out of me. They also kept hitting me with a wooden stick. All the people who were locked up inside the cages were screaming at them to stop hitting me with the wooden sticks and kicking me with their boots. The people kept shouting that the SKS wanted to kill Africa.

I lay face down on the floor and could not turn over. My joints hurt horribly, and there was no one to help me. They had already locked all the other undocumented guys up in those small cages.

While they were torturing me, I lay on the floor and told them I would remember all their faces and that they would not get away with what they did to me. I told them that when my lawyer came back from his honeymoon, I would make a case against them.

When they heard me mention the name "lawyer," they got nervous and started running out of the room. The next day, one of the SKS officers came to me. He had one star on his uniform and was among the officers who beat me up. He said he heard me saying that I had a lawyer.

The SKS officer asked me why I had been inside the Foreigners' Barracks for so long if I had a lawyer, and asked about the pain I complained of, but I kept silent. He said if I had told them from the beginning that I had a lawyer, they would have not touched me. He also asked me if I had taken any medicine, and I said no. He then called a doctor for me.

The next day, two nurses came in a small van and told the guard that they were looking for an African guy. The moment they saw me, they told me that their doctor wanted to see me. They said that one of the SKS officers told the doctor about me, and that their clinic was inside the jail. I then climbed into their van, and they took me to the doctor.

When I saw the doctor, he asked me some questions, including why I was in the Foreigners' Barracks. The doctor never checked my body. He just said that the SKS officer told him I couldn't sleep well.

I told the doctor that the same guys who called him on the phone beat me up, but the doctor didn't react. The doctor gave me some medicine, and he told me to take it at night, that the pills would help me sleep well.

I knew nothing about medicine, but I thank God that there was an African guy whom Immigration had brought that evening to the barracks. The guy's name was Victor.

Victor had been living in Italy for five years. The day he visited Curaçao, Immigration at the airport told him that his passport photo didn't look like him. So, they sent him to the Foreigners' Barracks. Immigration told him they didn't have any money to put him in a hotel, and he was supposed to go back to Italy the next day.

Victor shared the same room with me, and he had studied medicine in school. I told him I just came back from the prison clinic. I showed him the pills that the doctor gave me, and Victor shouted that those pills were for mad people, that they would only make me sleep, stay quiet, and forget many things.

I went to the toilet and flushed the pills away.

In the Foreigners' Barracks, we were so afraid for our lives each time the bad immigration officers or the guys from the SKS came. There was one guy from Santo Domingo who was staying in the barracks with us. One day, when the immigration officers brought more people into the Foreigners' Barracks, the guy was sitting on the desk outside, and he started calling out to one of the immigration officers to ask him how long they would keep him inside there.

The officer ignored his question, and the guy screamed at the officers that they should come and take him out of there. One of the immigration officers jumped on top of the desk where the guy was sitting and kicked his head like a football. He hit his head on the wall and passed out. The officers left him on the floor. He later regained consciousness, thank God.

Victor and I were shocked to witness that. It was like what they did to me.

I also tried to contact a friend of my uncle who was living in Curaçao while I was still inside the barracks. My uncle had given me the man's phone number hoping that maybe he could help me.

When the man discovered that I was calling him from the Foreigners' Barracks, he changed his phone number, because he was living in Curaçao illegally and didn't want any problems.

CHAPTER 27

My Lawyer Reappears

WHILE I WAS INSIDE THE Foreigners' Barracks, there were corrupt officers, but there were also good ones who were very kind to me. There was one SKS officer named Faustina. He was a very kind man. Anytime he was on duty, he came to me, and he always called me "brother." Faustina was born in Curaçao, and all his family are from the island. My situation bothered him.

Faustina would put his hand on the window, and he would pray for me. He would always encourage me to stay strong with God, and he also told me that his church was praying for me.

The food that they gave us inside the barracks was not so good, but these officers bought many nice things for me with their money.

I spent most of my time reading my Bible and learning how to read, write, and spell words because I always had a big problem with that.

I also did some exercises to keep myself busy and take my mind off my problems. The people who were inside the Foreigners' Barracks kept me company, but they came and went, while I had to stay for seemingly months unending.

The barracks became my home, and my freedom was locked up. I could only see Curaçao from the window.

After six months, my lawyer came to see me, and I was very mad at him for keeping me waiting for so long. The lawyer told me that he was very busy with some cases, and that he got married too, which was the reason he couldn't see me.

I told him all that I had been going through. Tired of staying there, I asked him how long it would be before I got my freedom.

The lawyer told me why my case was delayed. He said the government paid him five Antillean guilders, which is equivalent to three dollars an hour, anytime he visited me, and that he had other cases that paid him good money, which he needed to take care of before my case. He also told me he had received my passport and that the only way he could help me was for me to look for a way to pay him for my case.

He said he was working for the government, but if I could pay him 1,500 US dollars, he would speed up my case. He said this knowing that I was not working, and that I was only a "prisoner."

I asked him about the two police officers who helped me to stay in Curaçao. The lawyer told me he knew little about the officers, but he knew a certain African woman from Ghana. He said she'd lived in Curaçao for seventeen years. She could help contact people for me because he was busy with cases.

I took the woman's phone number from the lawyer, and I called her twice to let her know about my situation in the Foreigners' Barracks.

CHAPTER 28

An Appointment with the Court of Law

ON ONE OF THE DAYS that I called the woman from Ghana on her phone, I gave her the information of the two police officers from the seaport who helped me so she could look for them. She looked for them, but according to her, she couldn't find them.

She told me that she heard that the officers I sought had retired from their jobs. When I asked her about their chief of seaport police, she said he had retired too.

For over a month, I was so worried. All I could think about was how to get along with my lawyer, but in my spirit, I felt uncomfortable with the lawyer.

I was asking myself whether I had the right lawyer to defend me because I wouldn't be happy if they sent me back to Africa after all I had gone through.

Inside the Foreigners' Barracks, many of the undocumented immigrants who heard about my case didn't want to see Immigration deport me back to Africa. They gave me all kinds of advice about what to do and how to deal with my situation. At that moment, I called the lawyer on his office phone because I was so scared and confused; I asked him to visit me.

Before I left Dakar, I had 600 US dollars. I had made a small hole in my belt and put the money inside it. The belt was always on my waist. I told the lawyer to come with my passport. I didn't trust him again because I had a bad feeling that he was working with the immigration authorities.

Eight months had passed, and I didn't have my freedom yet. It appeared that my situation was getting worse. My spirit was so troubled.

I told the lawyer that I had 600 US dollars with me, and we made a deal. He took the money from me. I told him he'd get the rest of the money when he brought the case to court. But I really didn't know how I was going to pay him the rest of his money, and he never asked me from where I'd borrowed that kind of money to pay him.

I asked him to give me my international passport, and he asked me why I needed it. I told the lawyer that this international passport was all I had for now, so I wanted to keep it with me for a while. He gave it to me and left the Foreigners' Barracks.

I was confused about what to do with my Nigerian passport and was told by some people I met inside the Foreigners' Barracks that with this passport, Immigration would send me back to Africa. I didn't know what to do. I ran into the toilet, cut it into pieces, and flushed it away.

Around the eight-month mark, the SKS security officers at the Foreigners' Barracks came and opened the door for me. They told me I had to come to their office, that the lawyer wanted to speak with me on their office phone.

I spoke with the lawyer, and he told me he had fixed a date for my case in court. It was not good news to me. I had thought he would tell me that they would soon release me. I told him once again that I needed my freedom, to please help release me from this prison where they had kept me for eight months.

He told me to calm down, that he was doing the best he could, and that if I needed my freedom, I had to work with him. While we were talking on the phone, I told him that the court date he set was too soon for me. I didn't know what to tell the judge if the case went to court.

The lawyer told me that before I went to court, he'd visit me so we could talk about the case. When the security officers put me back in my cell, I became worried because I didn't know what would be on the mind of the judge.

CHAPTER 29

My Day in Court

ONE MORNING, THE LAWYER CAME to visit me, and I told him I didn't know what to tell the judge. I asked him, "What if the judge asked me my name and where I was born? What would I tell him now that I had changed the information on my case file?"

My lawyer told me I should not worry, that the judge wouldn't ask those questions. But the lawyer said he had told the judge everything about me; the judge would only tell Immigration to release me.

I told the lawyer that I'd heard all he said, but I asked one more time, "What if the judge asked me to tell the court who I was?" The lawyer responded that the judge wouldn't ask me to stand, and that he'd be there to defend me.

Two weeks after I spoke with my lawyer, the chief of immigration and police came to the Foreigners' Barracks. I asked him how long I would have to stay there. He looked at me and asked, "What were you thinking when you decided to remain in Curaçao?" He said he didn't even know who told the harbor authorities to keep me in Curaçao, and that he would ensure I was sent back to Africa.

I had been inside the barracks for eight months now and was still hoping that the government of Curaçao would free me.

He told me he wouldn't keep me in Curaçao—that Curaçao was not Holland, which gave people the right to live in the Netherlands.

What the chief of immigration and police said was not true, because I had met two Cuban guys who were there before me. The two Cuban guys got their freedom seven months after Immigration had locked them up. They released them because the government of Cuba didn't want the two guys to come back. Cuban law stated that if any Cuban citizen stayed outside of Cuba for over three months, they could not return to Cuba.

I wondered if the chief of immigration knew about the freedom of the two Cuban guys and that I'd stayed longer than they had. I told the chief that an officer told me that Immigration didn't have the power to deport me back to Africa, that before they could deport me, a judge had to decide.

I asked him if he knew that from the first day I jumped off the ship and my feet touched Dutch land, under Dutch law, I was protected. And that was what the officer told me.

The chief of immigration became angry and asked me who the officer was who passed such information to me. He said, of course, everyone wanted to live in Curaçao, to enjoy its good life, and that it was the reason I came to Curaçao.

I said, "Chief, honestly, I knew nothing about Curaçao. I'd never heard of it." I told him that it was when I was on the ship that I heard the name "Curaçao" for the first time. I looked it up on the map and couldn't find it. He asked what my original destination was. I said, "Europe, but unfortunately, the ship came to Curaçao, which was not my plan, but I would like to stay here in Curaçao if I get the opportunity."

He responded that he was looking for any official document to send me away, and that my ship was coming back to Curaçao soon. He said it would be easier for him to just put me back on board and end the matter there. I could barely hear another word from him; I was so shocked.

The chief left angrily, saying that *he* made the law in the Foreigners' Barracks, not the Dutch government.

When I was in the Foreigners' Barracks, I was told that the Dutch government gives the immigration authorities of Curaçao a lot of money to take care of the barracks. But Immigration never took care of it—the inside looked so horrible, and the infrastructure was bad.

I heard that part of the money that was given to Immigration by the Dutch government was used to buy tickets to send the undocumented people out of Curaçao instead of rebuilding the place.

But Immigration never bought tickets for the undocumented persons with this money. If the undocumented people didn't buy their own ticket with their own money, they had to stay for a very long time in the barracks, until one of their family members bought the ticket back home and sent it to Immigration for them.

One evening, Immigration called the office at the Foreigners' Barracks, and they told the security guard to inform me that my case would go to court the next day, so I needed to be ready.

When I got that message, I couldn't sleep. That was the first time in my life I would be going to any court.

I was also afraid of what the judge would say. The chief of immigration already told me he'd make sure that I was deported out of Curaçao.

The next day, Immigration came with their car to the Foreigners' Barracks. I asked them about my lawyer and said that I couldn't go to court without him because I didn't know what to tell the judge.

Immigration told me that my lawyer was waiting for me in the courtroom. They handcuffed me and took me to the court.

While we were on the road to the court, I got the opportunity for the first time to really see what Curaçao was like after over eight months. Willemstad, the capital of Curaçao, is the historic center and the most photographed place on the island. It is a beautiful Caribbean island and a colorful paradise with great infrastructure, plenty of nature to explore, and a lot of colorful buildings.

When we got to the courthouse, my lawyer was not there, so we had to wait until he came. I understood nothing they were saying in the court because they were speaking Dutch.

There was a lady who stood by my side. She was translating what the judge was saying from Dutch to English. The judge was a Dutchman, and he spoke English, but most of the time, everything was spoken in Dutch.

I was happy that, for the first time in eight and a half months, the government was paying attention to my case.

The lawyer had told me that he was there to defend me, and he also said that the judge would not ask me any questions. That lawyer was one of the worst lawyers I had ever seen in my life. The lawyer didn't even stand up in the courtroom. He didn't speak to me. He wasn't even sitting close to me.

The lady who was translating came and asked me if I understood what the judge was saying. I told her no, that I didn't understand the language. She was the only person who was close to me in the courtroom.

The lawyer was sitting so far from me, I couldn't ask him any questions, and he wasn't looking at me. I had destroyed my international passport, not knowing the lawyer had a copy of my passport with him for over four months, even though I asked him the day he brought it to me in the Foreigners' Barracks if he had any other copies, and he had said no.

Unknown to me, the lawyer had taken a copy of my passport and given it to the judge. That day in court, I was all alone, with Immigration sitting a little farther from me. They were hoping to take me back to Africa.

When the judge asked me to stand up, I almost shat myself. I asked the judge, "Who?" The judge said yes, that he was talking to me—and the judge was speaking in English. He told me to tell the court what my name was. Honestly, I couldn't handle it. I didn't know that the copy of my passport was in front of him. The judge said to me that he saw that I had three or four nationalities and three names in my case file.

I stood up to tell the court my name and where I came from. My feet and hands started shaking because I was not expecting that the judge would ask me any questions. That was what my lawyer told me inside the Foreigners' Barracks.

I told the court that my name was Jerry and that I was born in Nigeria. The judge noticed I was not feeling comfortable and that my entire body was trembling.

He asked, "Mr. Jerry, are you all right? Why are you trembling?"

Tears were running out of my eyes. I couldn't say anything to the judge, and I started feeling sad when I remembered all that I went through on the high seas and in the Foreigners' Barracks.

Everything I told the judge in the court was true because he told me that he had my case file before I began to speak in court.

The judge said to me that I had four nationalities on file, and that was indeed what I told Immigration out of frustration.

The judge pulled out the copy of my passport; I was totally shocked to see it in the judge's hand. Immigration couldn't deport me because the lawyer didn't know where he kept the copy until he found it on the court date.

The judge was very mad with the Immigration. He told them they had broken Dutch law. The judge also told Immigration that they didn't have any right to keep me in the Foreigners' Barracks for over eight and a half months. Curaçao Immigration was supposed to know that anyone under detention should come to court within three months.

The judge was so angry, he ordered Immigration to stand up, and he asked them what the crimes were that I had committed to be locked up for over eight and a half months without taking me to the court.

The immigration officers became speechless. The judge said many things to the officers in the Dutch language, which I didn't understand. The judge didn't even allow the immigration lawyer to talk.

I was not the only one whom they kept a long time in the Foreigners' Barracks, but I was the only one who stayed much longer.

The judge called Immigration, and he gave them the copy of my passport. He also told Immigration that he was giving them five days to send me back to Nigeria. The officers said they needed more time, but the judge refused and said once again, "Only five days."

The two immigration officers took me outside the courtroom, and they started asking me, "Where did you keep your passport?" They told me they needed the original passport to take me home. One of them then said that they could work with the copy.

We were still standing outside the courtroom, when my lawyer came and stood with us. He looked like the devil himself.

The lawyer told me I should not be worried, that the judge gave Immigration only five days. As a lawyer, he knew that the five days the judge gave them was too little to arrange my papers.

I didn't want to believe anything the lawyer told me again. The lawyer told me he would be in court to protect me, yet he was there without saying one word to the judge.

They all hoped that the judge would send me back to Africa. While I was talking with Immigration, they told the lawyer to give us a few minutes so they could ask me some questions.

Immigration asked me to tell them the truth so they could make some papers for me so I could stay in Curaçao. They wanted to know if I'd like to stay in Curaçao if they gave me the opportunity.

The question sounded like a rich man asking a poor man, who had lost all hope, if he needed some money to feed his family after eight and a half months.

I told Immigration, "Yes, of course, I'd love to stay in Curaçao if they'd let me." I also told them that if they didn't want me to stay in Curaçao, they should take me to Africa immediately, but I vowed I'd return to them. If they took me to Nigeria, I'd tell Nigerian Immigration that the passport was not mine.

The two immigration officers started talking to each other in their language. They put me back in their car and took me back to the Foreigners' Barracks. When their car arrived at the barracks, all the undocumented people who were locked inside there were happy to see me. They thought I'd been sent away to Africa.

CHAPTER 30

Awaiting Deportation from Curaçao

THE JUDGE WAS EXPECTING US in five days if they were unable to deport me. I lost my appetite. I found solace only in prayers and calling on God to help me. It seemed like all my dreams were about to come to an ugly end. I cried from the morning till the evening, yet there was no one who could help me.

Whenever I closed my eyes to sleep, I would get right into a terrible dream. All I could see in my dreams was that they sent me back to Africa, and that I couldn't leave again. This was not a great encouragement to me seeing that from a religious point of view I believed in the potency of dreams.

So, I could only cry to comfort myself. The undocumented people staying there with me all came together, encouraging me to have faith in God. It was a very painful experience that I had in the Foreigners' Barracks. Indeed, I cannot really explain all that had happened to me there in this book.

Two days had passed, with three days to go.

I was fasting and saying my prayers, hoping for a breakthrough, and didn't even notice the noise others were making. I couldn't hear anything people were saying. I looked at them while they were talking, but I didn't hear them because my mind was not there. I could only look out the window to see if the Immigration car was on its way coming—a sight loathed. I kept on praying, asking God to change the mind of the Immigration or the government.

I knew I was missing my parents back in Africa, but they wouldn't want to see me in an unpleasant situation because there was nothing they could do to help me.

European and Asian countries have deported thousands of people from different countries around the world. Some of them came home and took their own lives because of what they went through.

I acknowledge you're always responsible for your own happiness and success. Yes, life throws crap at you, but it is how you deal with it that really matters. I had learned many things from my past, and I was already making good plans for the future.

I had three more days to spend in the Foreigners' Barracks, and some of the undocumented people who were locked up told me I needed to escape because Immigration would deport me.

I didn't have any courage to escape because within my first five months' stay at the Foreigners' Barracks, four undocumented people from Jamaica escaped from there. It took the security officers only an hour to catch them all.

On the third night, I woke up, and I became so totally confused, I started hitting the door. All the security guards came out and started yelling at me, "Africa, stop! Africa, stop!," but I kept on hitting on the door.

The security officers became angry, and they started talking to each other, saying that this African guy had stayed so long inside the barracks that he was now going mad. What they did not know was that every time I woke up, I would be happy and grateful to God that I was still in that same Foreigners' Barracks and not on my way back to Africa.

CHAPTER 31
Arrival of the White Jeep

THEY SAY THAT THE BEST things always happen to those who are in the right place at the right time. While they still had me locked up in Curaçao, I made some calls to Senegal.

The only news I got was that one "pilot" whom I knew went to Europe successfully. He hid in a ship, and within seven days, he was already in Europe. I didn't know why my journey was different. I was begging God every minute to stop the Immigration's deportation plans against me.

The lawyer was nowhere to be found. I called his office, but there was no one to pick up the phone. Every time I saw a white Jeep drive past the Foreigners' Barracks, I became afraid and felt sick to my stomach. The color of the Immigration car was white, and so, throughout my five-day waiting period, I never enjoyed seeing a white Jeep pass by.

The third day passed, and they didn't show up. I kept on praying, and I was saying to God, "Please, there are only two days left. Please keep me strong." My prayers were a bit noisy as I kept at it, walking up and down in my room. Some of the undocumented immigrants also joined me in prayer.

On the fourth day, on the morning of February 9, 2001, the Immigration came to the Foreigners' Barracks in their white Jeep to pick me up. When I saw them arrive . . . I don't even know how to express how I felt that day in words. I thought my world was over. Darkness covered my eyes, and I became so sad that I wanted to kill myself.

Immigration started yelling, "Africa, Africa, pack your bag! You're going back to your country." I kept silent, and they kept on yelling, "Africa, pack your bag; you're leaving the Foreigners' Barracks today."

I had no energy to pray again. I could only say in my heart, "Father, if this is your wish to send me back to Africa, then I will go back to Africa, but please do not ask me how I spend my life anymore." I said again to God, "If this plan wasn't yours, please let me stay in Curaçao."

Immigration came inside and took my bag, and as I was going with them, I didn't know what to say again. At that moment, in the whole Foreigners' Barracks, which was full of so many people, there was an enormous silence.

Some people were shouting, "Africa!," while others were crying for me, saying that this man had stayed inside here for nine months. I didn't care anymore. I kept on walking with them to their car. But before I reached it, I turned back and looked at the Foreigners' Barracks, where I had been locked up for nine months.

I felt so much emotion and started crying when I remembered all that I went through and all that happened while I was there. Immigration told me, "Africa, be strong."

They put me inside their car, but this time they didn't put handcuffs on me. They drove away.

While they were driving, I asked one of them where they were taking me. The man said they were taking me to the airport. I started trying to figure out how to escape from the car, but this was difficult because I was sitting in between the two officers.

I said to myself that if I got to the airport and they tried to put me on the airplane, I would jump out and run. Many thoughts were going through my head. In fact, I was so worn out that I truly couldn't plan anything at that moment.

Immigration told me I shouldn't be worried about going back to Africa, that my country would be pleased to welcome me, that I should be happy I was going home, but I kept silent.

CHAPTER 32

Freedom!

I UNDERSTAND THAT THERE ARE many opportunities in life, but sometimes they don't come around easily. To me, this was the best opportunity for me to settle down overseas. In life, things you hope on or believe in could disappoint you. All I know is that God will forsake no one who trusts in him. When you have doubts and questions, fears and struggles, be honest about it—faith doesn't exempt you from the trials of life, and faith doesn't make you not to feel things. I have come to understand, when you're honest with God about your doubts, your shortcomings, and your fears, it's not a weakness. Indeed, it is strength when you humble yourself and ask God for help. He will give you grace to overcome what you could not overcome, and that was exactly what I did.

While we were on the road, heading to a place I did not know, the immigration officers received a call, and they turned their car around and drove to their office in the city. They took me inside the office and went into another office, while I was sitting waiting for them.

I nodded off because they kept me in their office for over three hours. I couldn't run because the entire office was locked. After those three hours, they came out, and they told me they were in a meeting. But they didn't tell me who they were talking to.

One of the immigration officers called out to me, "Africa." I answered him, and he told me I was a free man.

I didn't understand what he was saying at the moment because he was laughing, and I know that Immigration doesn't like to free people in captivity—Oh yes, they loved deportation. The officer said again that they had released me and that I was a free man. He told me I could live in Curaçao as long as I wanted, but they had a problem, which was where to keep me.

The officer asked me if I knew any Africans who were living in Curaçao, and that maybe I could stay with them. I told the immigration officer that I knew one African woman who was living in Curaçao who came from Ghana.

The officer asked if I could contact her to come there and sign for me so I could go with her. I was so happy. I forgot all my pain and problems from Dakar to Spain and from there to Curaçao. At that moment, I felt so happy and started asking myself if this was the freedom I had been dreaming of for such a long time now. All the immigration officers were looking at me as I was jumping up and down and praising God.

I said that I would always proclaim God's mighty acts and his sovereignty. The Almighty God did such a noble thing in my life. While I was in the Foreigners' Barracks, I thought I was alone in Curaçao, without knowing that the Most High God had good plans for me.

I called the woman from Ghana on the phone and told her I was in the immigration office in the city. She was so happy to hear that I was finally free from the Foreigners' Barracks, and she said she was on her way to come and see me.

While I was still in the immigration office in the district called Punda, I noticed that some of the officers were not happy that I was free from the Foreigners' Barracks. It was either that, or they wanted to see me thrown out of Curaçao. The ones who were happy with me really wanted to know more about African history, hoping that one day they'd visit the motherland.

They were also curious to know more about me. I did not know where to start talking about myself. So, I told my story to the immigration officers—to the ones who were happy—that I had been released.

I told them that since I was born, I had always been a person who was positive about every aspect of life—that there was much more that I would like to experience. I told them that I liked to hear the Word of God and read the Bible—that I liked to dream, and this was the best part of my life.

Some of the immigration officers were happy to hear from me when I told them about myself because they knew that for the last nine months, I couldn't talk to some of them because I was in such great pain. In their office, most of the immigration officers wanted to visit Africa. The two immigration officers who wanted to take me to the airport also told me that they too had visited Africa before. They'd gone to Lagos, Nigeria, because a couple of years ago there were two African guys who were in Curaçao illegally. Immigration officers caught them at a construction company where they were working. They sent the two African guys to the Foreigners' Barracks, but the two guys couldn't handle the conditions inside there. They broke things that were inside there and made a lot of noise the whole day.

The SKS police security officers who were on guard at the Foreigners' Barracks that day became angry and called the two immigration officers who came to take me to the airport. When the two immigration officers came to the Foreigners' Barracks, they were not happy to see the way the two African guys were behaving. They became so angry and started shouting at them. The two African guys made it clear to Immigration that they didn't want to stay inside the barracks one more day.

The two immigration officers told me they didn't touch those guys. But it was a surprise to see what the two African guys did. They said these guys picked up a broken bottle and cut their hands and faces. The two officers said that the moment they saw what the guys were doing to themselves, they ran back to their office and reported what they just saw. Within a few days, the two African guys' cases went to court.

When they were in court, the two guys told the judge that the two immigration officers cut their bodies with a broken bottle, but Immigration told the judge that was not true.

The two officers told me that the judge was angry about the whole situation, and he ordered the immigration department to pay the two African guys 5,000 Netherlands Antillean guilders each and send them back to Africa, where they came from.

The two guys got paid, but Immigration had to go on the flight with them to Lagos, Nigeria, in West Africa. That was how the two officers visited Lagos.

When the two officers finished telling their story to me, I felt sorry for them. But it appeared that the two officers were still looking for a way to avenge what the two guys did to them in the court.

Even though they had used the situation to visit Africa, the officers were still unhappy. The two African guys had stayed in the

Foreigners' Barracks for just a few days before Immigration took their case to court.

On the other hand, I spent nine months inside the Foreigners' Barracks without Immigration taking me to court. And I don't know the reason why they didn't bring me back to the court like the judge said, within five days, if they couldn't send me back to Africa.

It appeared that the immigration department was afraid that the judge would order them to pay me a lot for keeping me over nine months in the Foreigners' Barracks. In my case, they couldn't give the judge a reason why they kept me so long before bringing me to the court, and that was why they were speaking with me.

While I was at their office in Punda, Willemstad, chatting with them, the woman from Ghana arrived at the office. She came inside and asked for me. That day was the first time I saw her. We had only spoken on the phone.

The immigration department asked the Ghanaian woman if she could sign for me so I could stay with her. She was happy that I had finally gotten my freedom. She signed the papers, and I went home with her. Before we left, Immigration told me I had to come to their office every four days to sign a paper to attest that I was still in Curaçao.

Immigration gave me a paper written in Dutch, which they stamped. They told me if the police stopped me, I should show that paper to them. The paper was a temporary Curaçao permit. They also told me I could not work; they just put me on the street to suffer and probably die.

I asked them if they could take me back to the judge so the judge could see my condition, but they refused. I haven't been happy with the immigration department of Curaçao to date because they released me from the Foreigners' Barracks and put the responsibility of taking care of me on the Ghanaian woman. They didn't even ask her how she would support me while I was living in her house, and they were the ones who told me to contact her.

The Ghanaian woman had an African souvenir shop in Curaçao, but her merchandise was not moving well. It was a painful thing that she was using her money to support me, while I was strong enough to work and feed myself.

Every four days I had to go to Immigration so they could see that I was still in Curaçao. I tired of asking the Ghanaian woman to help me while I could work and get what I wanted for myself.

For a couple of months, I'd been going to Immigration just to show myself to them. One day, I became very angry, and I went to the immigration office in Punda. I told them I needed a job. I kept on telling them I needed permission to work and a permanent permit to show that I was living in Curaçao. Yet, they refused to give it to me.

The immigration officers told me I should stop coming to their office and stop signing the papers I used to sign when I visited their office. They told me they knew I was in Curaçao, so I should stop coming to their office to disturb them about how I would survive if they refused to give me a work permit.

The officers kept silent thereafter. I didn't know what more to do, so I left their office. I went to look for a job, but I couldn't find anyone who would take me because I didn't have a Curaçao work permit.

Since I left from the Foreigners' Barracks, things were not going well for me, so I went back again to the immigration office.

But this time I met with the new chief officer. He didn't even care to hear me out. The only thing that he said to me was that I should thank God that I was in Curaçao. He also told me that were it left to him, he would have put me back aboard the day the ship arrived in Curaçao.

CHAPTER 33

The Agony of Work without Work Permit

FOR A LONG TIME, I didn't show up at the immigration office again. While I was still living with the Ghanaian woman, I met two African guys who came to Curaçao to sell their African souvenirs. When they sold all their souvenirs, they stayed in Curaçao.

The two guys found an apartment that had two rooms, one small and one big. So, I asked them if I could take the small room and stay with them. They agreed to give it to me. I went to the Ghanaian woman. I pleaded with her to help me pay for the room, and she graciously did.

I started living together with the two African guys. The three of us were undocumented in Curaçao because none of us had the Curaçao resident permit.

I kept on looking for a place to work because I had to pay my rent and feed myself. I found a security company, and they would take me. But what they were paying me was too small because I had no work permit.

I had no choice but to accept the little money the security company was paying me. I needed to work to take care of myself.

In Dakar, my uncle and his family were happy that they released me from the Foreigners' Barracks. Alice also was happy to hear that they had released me. After a couple of months, Alice met a white man who lived in Spain, and he took Alice there.

One night, I was where the security company posted me when Alice called me on my mobile phone. She was so happy to tell me she was going to get married to the white man who took her to Spain. That was the last time I heard from her.

On February 26, 2001, I got another job in a company called Price Right. I was working there as well as at the security company. I used to work at Price Right from 7:30 a.m. to 6:00 p.m. After I stopped working at 6:00 p.m., I changed my clothes and took a bus to the security company. At the security company, my work normally started at 6:30 p.m. and stopped at 7:00 a.m. I never rested for a day; I was working from Monday to Sunday.

There were many good jobs in Curaçao, but you need a work permit to get those jobs. Price Right was an enormous store that sold refrigerators and all kinds of stuff. My job was to arrange and rearrange their warehouse and to deliver goods to the customers.

I became tired from working two jobs without a day off. One night, while I was where the security company posted me, I became so exhausted and felt very sleepy, and I started looking for a place to take a quick nap.

I was guarding an ice-cream company in a dangerous neighborhood that night. I went inside a truck, and the entire gate at the company yards were locked, but somehow, some bad guys climbed over the gate.

I was lucky that they did not kill me that night. They opened the front of the truck in which I was sleeping and removed some parts.

I thank God that I survived because I wouldn't have lived to tell my story.

I called the security company on my walkie-talkie from 4:38 a.m. to 6:48 a.m., but they didn't come. When the security guard arrived to pick me up, they told me that their car broke down, which was why they couldn't come when I was calling.

I did not want to guard the ice-cream company again, and the security company posted me to another place. This time the security company gave me one of their best giant K9 dogs to guard with—his name was Awesome. We were guarding a school compound that was at the back of a wide cemetery yard.

It scared me to guard there at night. At midnight, the entire area felt very creepy. The crazy giant K9 dog they gave me was no fun at all. It loved to sleep from evening to morning. Most nights the dog would leave me all alone in the school compound and would hide where it would be difficult for me to find him, and have a good night's sleep. The dog was mostly eating and sleeping.

But I, however, felt safe guarding the school because I knew the K9 dog they gave me was around somewhere. I really hoped it showed up whenever the situation demanded his presence. Nevertheless, I was scared of getting too close to the dog because it was a vicious K9 dog. It was crazy enough to bite even its owners.

CHAPTER 34

Sad News from Dakar

Within a couple of months, I stopped working at the security company, and Price Right remained the only company that I was working for. One day, I wrote a letter to the governor and told her I was having difficulty living in Curaçao without a resident permit.

In a couple of months, I miraculously got my permit. I was still working at Price Right. I lived in a neighborhood called Santa Maria. One day, I got information that one of the Curaçao seaport police officers who helped me to stay in Curaçao was living on the same street as I. His name was Mr. Arnold. I went to look for him, and when I got to his house, he was both shocked and happy to see me.

Mr. Arnold told me that one of his friends had informed him about my release the day I was released from the Foreigners' Barracks. I asked him about the other officer who was working with him (his name was Jerry).

Mr. Arnold told me that Mr. Jerry, he, and their chief of seaport police had retired from their job. I felt so sorry for them, and I asked him the reason they retired.

Mr. Arnold apologized that they did not show up again after I was put in the Foreigners' Barracks. He also told me they retired within a month while I was in the Foreigners' Barracks. They didn't like the way things were going on in the office.

He also told me that Mr. Jerry and their chief of seaport police had gone to Holland to live. He said that they were tired and angry about staying in Curaçao because of the way the Curaçao government was running their island.

I told him of the pain and suffering I had undergone while I was in the Foreigners' Barracks for nine months. I also told him how eight SKS police almost killed me inside the barracks, and that I thought that they were my friends, not knowing that some of them hated me.

Mr. Arnold became furious and told me that my case was one of the reasons they quit their job. I had a lawyer when I was there, but the lawyer couldn't do anything when I told him what the SKS police officers did to me.

Mr. Arnold was not happy with the entire story I told him, and he said he knew that the lawyer I had when I was in the Foreigners' Barracks was not the one they sent to me.

Mr. Arnold told me that those SKS officers would not go free for what they did to me because it was against the law in Curaçao and Holland. He took me to a friend of his who was a lawyer. Mr. Arnold explained everything that I told him to the lawyer, and he asked the lawyer to help me fight my case. He also told the lawyer that what Immigration did was not good, that they would have taken me back to the judge when they saw they couldn't deport me back to Africa.

Mr. Arnold told the lawyer that he knew what the judge would have done to the immigration department, and that was the reason they didn't send me back to the judge.

The lawyer was among the best lawyers on the Curaçao island. He said he'd fight the Immigration and the SKS police officers. He also told me I could win my case, and the government would have to pay me a lot of money for what they did to me in the Foreigners' Barracks.

The lawyer asked me if I wanted to stay in Curaçao because they might send me out of Curaçao when the government paid me. The lawyer told me that it was only if I became a citizen of Curaçao or got Dutch nationality that the government would not send me out of Curaçao if they paid for what they did to me.

I had no other choice than to leave the case alone because I didn't want to be in a situation in which they would send me away after all. The lawyer told me that there were more opportunities for me if I stayed there in Curaçao. If fighting the case was not the right thing to do at that moment, then the right time would come.

Mr. Arnold told me that what the lawyer said was true, so we went back to his house, and he gave me the phone number of his partner, Mr. Jerry, to call him and say hello.

The next day I called Mr. Jerry's phone number in Holland, and it thrilled him to hear from me. He was not planning to come back to Curaçao again.

Within a couple of days, I went back to see Mr. Arnold, but his son told me he had moved to Bonaire. His son gave me his phone number to contact him. When I contacted Mr. Arnold in Bonaire, he told me I should move to Bonaire, that he knew a company that was giving away jobs. I told him that I had a job at Price Right and preferred to keep on working there.

Before 2001 ended, I met Brigitte, a Dutch lady who worked with me at the same company, Price Right. Brigitte was born in

Holland, and she was a painter by profession. She loved to paint signs and children's rooms. She had been in Curaçao for a long time. I went out with her, and she took me to many places that I had never been to in Curaçao. She was funny, kind by nature, and beautiful and understanding, and the company where we worked knew that we were in love.

After some months, I moved in together with her and her two children in a house in Curaçao. In early 2003, I stopped working at Price Right, and we opened up our own souvenir shop in the city of Punda. In the middle of that year, 2003, I got a message from Senegal that my uncle Chika was in the hospital in Dakar with a kidney problem. Within two days of my getting the message, my uncle died.

When I got the sad news that he died, it devastated me because since I met my uncle in Senegal, I knew him as a vigorous man and a healthy person. I was waiting for the day that I could travel to Nigeria to tell my parents how I met him in Senegal, and he promised we would travel together to Nigeria. I couldn't believe that he died. I remembered him and the life we spent together in Dakar.

When I came out from the Foreigners' Barracks, my uncle had visited me in Curaçao. So, it was very painful to hear that he had left this world. I loved him so much.

His Senegalese wife got frustrated. She made some contacts in Nigeria by reaching out to my family with the help of some Nigerians living in Dakar.

My uncle hadn't seen his mother or talked to her for over twenty-four years. His death was very painful for the entire family. The reason he couldn't go back to Nigeria was not just because of Nigeria's problems. While he was alive, he had told me that he did not want to see his family in his present situation, because things were not going well with him financially in Dakar. He wanted to make some good money like some of his friends did before he could see his mother and the family.

It was unfortunate that he died while hoping for the day he would put a smile on the faces of his family members.

Some of his Nigerian friends who lived in Senegal helped his wife. They took his body back to Nigeria, and that was the first time his wife visited Nigeria. It was heartbreaking news for the entire family back home—he left many years ago, and the family was expecting him to return to the village alive, not in this ugly situation.

Many Africans living all over the world had the similar issues like my uncle had. Some of them had stayed so long abroad that they had forgotten the road leading to their houses in their villages because they were yet to achieve their dreams overseas. Some of them had been living overseas for over thirty years and had never traveled to visit their homeland within this period.

CHAPTER 35
Tales of Woe from Nigeria

NIGERIA HAS A CULTURE THAT is terrible and is killing many Nigerian youths. This stupid culture is centered on money and the associated pride of life that our forefathers passed onto our parents. As a result, some of our parents have been putting heavy burdens on the shoulders of their children.

This is one of the reasons that many Nigerians can't return to Nigeria. Thousands of Nigerians want to make lots of money before they return home, and before they know it, thirty or thirty-five years would have elapsed. Time just flies, and they are left wondering how it just seems like yesterday that they left Nigeria.

Yes, many people make an honest living, but there are also those who are dishonest. These are mostly the ones who make their money in a bad way and go to Nigeria to show off. Many Nigerian parents, when they see how the ones who come back from overseas are misusing money in the city and in the villages, out of poverty and hardship, call their children and put pressure on them to make quick money. The ones who have lived overseas for many years become scared and ashamed to come back home because they do not have illicit money to spend.

Most of these Nigerians who live overseas become frustrated from the great responsibility and pressure our parents put on them. The frustrated ones are the dangerous ones because they are now ready to kill even their own brother if he stands between them and making money. Some of them go into drugs, fraud, and money laundering, and all these monetary proceeds are used for building their beautiful houses, buying their cars, and helping to take care of their families.

Most of these societal problems in Nigeria are caused by our greedy leaders who rule the country for their own selfish interests. The Nigerian government is corrupt, and many of our citizens in the diaspora have taken the law into their hands, trying to do what they can to help their loved ones survive the hardships of Nigeria.

Such was the case with my late uncle. He spent most of his life in Germany and Italy. They deported him from Italy to Senegal because of invalid documents, and he couldn't return to Europe again.

In 2003, when my uncle's wife came back to Nigeria, and they concluded my uncle's funeral, she called me and gave me the phone number of my parents so I could call and talk with them because she knew I hadn't spoken with them for a long time.

I was so happy to speak with my parents on the phone, and they were happy that I was living in Curaçao, wherever that was. They were just happy to hear that I was calling from overseas. I left Nigeria in the year 1996, and they hadn't heard from me again until I called them in 2003.

When I spoke to my father, I learned they were okay. My father told me on the phone about the problems that they had been facing in Nigeria from the day that the government shut down his office. He hoped that one day the Nigerian police force would pay him the money that they owed him for his service.

He told me some sad news, which was very painful for me. In the year 1996, when I left Nigeria, one of my nephews, Ikenna, traveled to Togo, one of the African countries. Ikenna went to Togo to meet a couple of his friends, but when he got there, his friends introduced him to the drug business.

They offered Ikenna 3,000 US dollars, which he couldn't resist. He only needed to do a couple of things for his friends before they would pay him. Ikenna's friends sent him to São Paulo, Brazil, to get drugs for them. I was told that my nephew went to Brazil twice for the drug business because he was looking for a way to support himself and help solve some problems that they had in their family.

When Ikenna got to Brazil, he stayed there without going back to Togo because he always said that he wanted to live overseas. My father said that on December 23, 1996, Ikenna came back from Brazil, and he sent a message to his parents that he was in a hotel in Lagos, Nigeria.

Ikenna told his parents that they should wait for him because they wanted to travel to the village on December 25, 1996. He told them he was coming to meet them in the city where they lived, on December 24, so they could travel together to the village and spend their Christmas there. His parents waited for him to come back like he said in the message he sent to them, but Ikenna never showed up.

Ikenna died the same day, on December 23, 1996, in the hotel room in Lagos. The drugs that he brought from Brazil exploded in his stomach because he could not excrete them out on time.

My parents and my nephew's parents were still waiting for Ikenna, but he did not show up on the twenty-fourth or the twenty-fifth, and on the twenty-sixth, my parents went to the village with Ikenna's parents.

It surprised them to see Ikenna's friends on December 28. They came to our village and told them he died on December 23, though they couldn't tell our parents what killed Ikenna. The Christmas that they were enjoying became a sorrowful day for them. Only after December did our parents find out how Ikenna died in the hotel in Lagos.

My father also told me that one of my uncles in Nigeria had died a couple of years back. His name was Mr. Walter, and he died of a heart attack because his first son lost all the money raised for him to travel to Europe.

He had sold the land that belonged to the whole family in Aba for thirteen million naira. Mr. Walter then gave the thirteen million naira to his first son who had told him he knew someone in Côte d'Ivoire, West Africa, who promised to help him get the right documents he needed to travel to Europe.

His son went to Côte d'Ivoire to meet his contact, but the whole thing was a scam. He lost everything. He didn't go to Europe, and when his father got the news, he was sad and heartbroken. My father told me that within three days, Mr. Walter had a heart attack and died in his house in Aba. His son refused to come back to Nigeria, not even to attend the burial occasion of his father.

All the news that my father gave me was heartbreaking, but what could I say to him?

In the middle of 2003, I called my late uncle's wife to find out how she was doing. She told me she was not happy because she loved my uncle so much. It surprised me to hear that comment from her. Honestly, I never knew that she was so in love with my uncle. She was so sad, and she wanted to go to Nigeria to see his family.

She said that my uncle always told her to wait until he made money. Then they would travel to Nigeria. He did not want his family in Nigeria to see him as a poor man.

In early 2004, I called Senegal, and they told me that Mary, my late uncle's wife, died. I was totally shocked when I got the painful news. A few people in Dakar said that it was my late uncle's spirit that took her life because of the way she treated him when he was alive, but I never believed their stories.

I think that Mary may have died from depression and the problems that she must have been facing in Senegal. I never want to visit Senegal again because I have nothing to look forward to or see there again.

CHAPTER 36
Finally, I Travel to Europe!

I WAS HAPPY TO GET the chance to stay in Curaçao, but I wasn't happy to hear of the problems that many Africans were facing from deportation all over the world.

On Tuesday, April 15, 2010, one hundred of Nigeria's citizens were deported from Johannesburg, South Africa. They arrived at Nigeria's international airport in Lagos—ninety-nine males and one female.

When I was in Dakar, the Nigerian government made a deal with some of the European countries—Switzerland, Belgium, Germany, Norway, France, and the Netherlands—to send back Africans who were living illegally in their countries. On another occasion, over one hundred Nigerians were dropped off in Gambia, a West African country, and were given twelve US dollars each and told to find their way home. I actually met with one of the people who was among those deported.

Many people living in Nigeria do not know all the problems that people who travel outside the country under such circumstances face. Our leaders took money from the European countries and agreed that Africans should be deported back to their motherland. This was very painful for us Africans who viewed ourselves as being under severe hardship foisted on us by several administrations of corrupt, insensitive, and reckless leadership.

In Sudan, they deported over eighty Nigerians in March 2010 because of immigration issues. I was told that in the same March, ninety Nigerians were deported from the United Kingdom.

Twenty-eight Nigerians were deported from Trinidad and Tobago in March 2010. In February 2010, Dublin, Ireland, also deported fifty-eight Nigerians because of immigration issues.

Libyan Immigration deported thousands of people to Nigeria every year, not knowing whether they were Nigerians or not. Spain deported over seventy Nigerians in 2009.

Many countries humiliated a lot of Africans with deportation. After they had spent so much time and energy, and all their money too, Immigration still deported them. Most of the guys deported back to Africa started living precariously. Curaçao and other Caribbean islands deported many Africans too. And so, all the sad news that I was hearing made me want to live a normal, self-respecting life while I was in Curaçao.

When I opened a souvenir shop in Punda, the Dutch woman whom I met as a coworker also stopped working for that company and joined me to run the souvenir shop. Our previous employer was so happy for me because I was a hard worker.

On November 14, 2003, I had my first son in Curaçao with Brigitte. It thrilled me to become a father, and I love my son, Chijioke, very much.

The souvenir business I opened wasn't doing so well in Curaçao, so I closed it down and opened up another business in the same building, selling leather Italian shoes. But before I could start the shoe business, I had to travel to Europe to buy my shoes, and I needed a visa to go to Europe.

Curaçao was under Holland's rule, but it was always a challenge to apply for a visa at the Dutch embassy in Curaçao. The first time I wanted to apply for a visa, I put in my application, and they denied it after seven days of waiting. Brigitte became angry because we needed to visit her parents in Holland. From there, we planned to travel to Italy to buy the shoes we wanted to sell in our shop. It was December 2003.

The Dutch embassy refused to put a visa on my passport because I came from Nigeria, and I had a Nigerian passport. The next day, when I returned to the Dutch embassy with Brigitte, she wanted to know why they refused the visa. At the Dutch embassy, Brigitte met the Dutch woman who told me I would not get a visa to travel to Europe.

The Dutch woman told us that if they put a visa on my passport, I wouldn't return to Curaçao, and Nigerians get into all kinds of trouble in Holland.

We told the Dutch embassy not to victimize us by denying me the visa because of the crimes Nigerians and other Africans commit in Europe. I was not happy about it.

We went back home, and I wrote a letter to one of the Dutch offices in Holland. In my letter, I explained everything that happened when I applied for a visa. Within a couple of weeks, they answered my letter in Holland, and the Dutch office in Curaçao called me back to pick up my visa.

I know this is the same problem most people face whenever they apply for a visa. I had never been to Europe before, and the day they approved my visa, I was so happy that finally I would visit Europe.

In December 2003, I visited Holland with Brigitte and my son. We spent a couple of days with her family, and from there, we went to Italy, and we spent five days in a hotel in Napoli. I also visited Victor, the African guy who saved me from taking the medicine in the Foreigners' Barracks. He lived in Napoli.

Victor had spent three months in the Foreigners' Barracks before the immigration officers sent him back to Italy. Victor could not believe it the day he saw me in Italy with Brigitte and my son.

While I was in Italy with Victor, he told me how he came to Italy. He left Nigeria for Italy in 1992, but life in Napoli was too difficult for him. He told me that while he was in Italy, his mother died, and he couldn't travel back to Nigeria because he had no money to pay for his ticket.

Within four years after his mother died, his father too died, but still Victor couldn't travel back to Nigeria to bury his father. He was afraid to travel to Nigeria because he didn't have the Italian permit yet. Victor was afraid that he might never come back to Europe. He was planning to live in Europe until he made money because he was an only son.

After five years, Victor got his Italian permit, but before Victor got the Italian permit, he went through hell. He told me that after he had lived in Italy for three years, the city where he was living became too tough to survive in. He wanted to leave the city for another European country, but he did not have a passport with him.

Victor met one American soldier in Napoli who needed money. They both met each other on a cruise ship that was going from Napoli to Rome. Victor needed a passport, so the American soldier sold his passport to Victor. He told Victor that he had to use the passport within two days, because after two days, he would declare that the passport was missing.

Victor took the passport and flew to France. When he arrived, they caught him at the airport with the forged passport. Victor tried to defend the passport and told French Immigration that he was born in America because Immigration was about to deport him.

French Immigration knew the passport did not belong to Victor. They told him that he spoke like an African. They then took the ID card and passport from him.

They asked Victor to tell them where he was from, but he refused to cooperate with them. Because he claimed he was born in America, French Immigration took Victor to the American embassy in Paris.

When they got to the American embassy, they met the consul, who asked Victor which state he said he was born in. Victor told the American consulate where he was born, and after a lengthy conversation, the American consulate first commended Victor for his "long" story but then told him that he was not born in the United States of America. The consul told French Immigration to take him out of his office.

Victor begged French Immigration to let him leave France, but they refused to let him go. They put pressure on him so he would tell them where he was born. Then he told them he was born in Senegal.

The next day, they took Victor to the Senegalese consulate in Paris, and Victor could not even speak French. The Senegalese consulate spoke to Victor in French and in Wolof, but Victor didn't understand what the man was saying.

The Senegalese consulate told French Immigration to try the Nigerian embassy, that Victor was not from Senegal. The next day, they took him to the Nigerian embassy. Immigration told the consul of Nigeria that the reason they brought Victor to his office was that they had been trying all the African embassies to find out where Victor was from.

The moment Victor spoke, the consul knew he was from Nigeria. The Nigerian consul started laughing because he saw Victor was angry and refused to claim his Nigerian citizenship.

Their consul told French Immigration to wait outside, that he wanted to speak with Victor alone. The consul told Victor that he knew he came from Imo State in Nigeria. The consul himself once lived in the state where Victor was born, so when Victor spoke, the consul knew that was the way they spoke in that city. Still, Victor refused to claim his Nigerian citizenship. He told him he had been living with Nigerians and other African people, which was why he spoke like that.

The consul told Victor that since he said that he was not a Nigerian, he should keep to that story. The Nigerian consul called French Immigration to take Victor from his office and said that he had tried to discern where Victor originated from, but that he refused to talk.

The consul also told Immigration to try another embassy in France. French Immigration became furious with Victor. They put him back on his flight, and they went back to Paris. When they got to their office, they were so angry that they put Victor in a room with no windows.

They told him to take his clothes off, and they put him in a building with no glass windows. It was freezing outside. Cold came in from all the open spaces, and his whole body was freezing.

After all their torture, he still did not confess that he was a Nigerian citizen. And so, within two days, they took Victor to the court, and the judge told Victor that he had twenty-four hours to leave France. The judge also told him that if they ever caught him again in France, he would jail him. French Immigration then allowed Victor to go.

When Victor left the court, he immediately ran down to a train station, but he had no money with him. He took off his gold necklace and sold it to an African lady whom he saw at the train station, after explaining his problem to her.

Victor used the money to buy his ticket back to Napoli, and after five years, he received his permit. I remember applying some lessons learned from some of his experiences that he narrated to me while I was in the Foreigners' Barracks, and it helped me a lot.

Brigitte and I spent four days in Napoli, and Victor took us to a place where I bought all the shoes I wanted to sell in my shop in Curaçao. We went back to Holland and spent two more days with Brigitte's family. Then we went back to Curaçao.

The Dutch embassy in Curaçao saw that I did not overstay in Europe. Indeed, I visited Europe twice while I was living in Curaçao.

The shoe shop I started in Curaçao went well until 2004, when many businesses closed down and some people moved their businesses to Saint Martin and Aruba.

Before the end of 2004, I closed down my shoe shop because European tourists were not coming to Curaçao the way they used to come. But I did well in Curaçao. Most European and American tourists had never heard of Curaçao, and they do not even know where it is located. However, Saint Martin, Aruba, Bonaire, and other Caribbean islands are well known.

The government of Curaçao was not doing much to expose Curaçao to the world to boost tourism, even though Curaçao is bigger and more beautiful than Saint Martin and some other Caribbean islands.

When I closed my shoe shop in Punda in 2004, I opened up another business in the same building. It is one of the biggest internet cafés in Punda. It's called Big Daddy Internet Café.

CHAPTER 37

The Fate of Foreigners' Barracks

IN 2005, THERE WAS A big problem.

Immigration was controlling the entire city of Curaçao—they were catching people on the streets and on the buses in Curaçao who were undocumented. They locked up all the people they caught inside the Foreigners' Barracks.

There were two African guys I knew in Curaçao who were among the people whom they caught. One of these guys used to visit my shop.

Immigration had deported all the people they caught on the streets. Only the two African guys were left there. One had a South African passport, and the other a Nigerian passport.

Immigration could not deport the one who had the South African passport, and they told him that the South African passport he had didn't belong to him. The one who had a Nigerian passport refused to give it to Immigration. He told them he lived in Colombia.

Immigration told the two African guys that both of them were Nigerians, and that if they didn't bring their passports, they would stay for a very long time inside the Foreigners' Barracks. So, their problems became worse in the Foreigners' Barracks, as Immigration abandoned the two of them completely for one year.

The government of Curaçao did not know that these guys were inside for over a year, and that they were not even taken to the court. When the office of Human Rights in Curaçao heard about them, they were not happy to get that kind of news. One of the African guys told me that a security officer in the Foreigners' Barracks had helped them by telling the Human Rights officials that they were inside there.

This was a big problem for Immigration. What they were doing in secret had finally come into the public square. They could no longer keep the illegal people inside the Foreigners' Barracks for more than three months without taking them to court. Human Rights in Curaçao told the Office of the Governor to free the two African guys they were holding.

Some of the Human Rights workers also visited the Foreigners' Barracks while the two African guys were still inside. It upset them how the place smelled, both inside and outside.

The next day, Immigration released the two African guys. The one who had a Nigerian passport did not have any place to stay. Immigration rented a room for him for a few months. Then they told him he was on his own, and that they were expecting both of them to leave Curaçao as soon as possible.

The Curaçao human rights organization asked Immigration why they couldn't fix the Foreigners' Barracks with the money the Dutch government gave them. It was such a big scandal. The human rights organization told the immigration department to close the Foreigners' Barracks until they could fix it. They said it was built like a place for animals, not people.

I hope they fix the Foreigners' Barracks because when I was there, it was a horrible place. They shut it down for a very long time, and the two African guys continued to live in Curaçao because Immigration refused to grant them the Curaçao permit.

CHAPTER 38

A Visit to Nigeria

In December 2005, I had my second son, Ifeanyi. I'm so happy to have two kids who call me "Papa." Every morning I wake up, I sing praises and worship the Almighty God for all He has done for me and my family.

In the same year, 2005, we planned to get married in Curaçao, but my documents were not complete, so I contacted my father to mail my papers so I could get married. My father tried hard to get all the papers I needed. It was difficult.

Before you can get married in Curaçao, you need to bring many documents, and in my country, Nigeria, most of our documents are awfully hard to find. The recordkeeping culture was poor, and there were no computers to store our documents in the early times of the nation. My father tried and sent all the documents that I needed.

It was very difficult to get all the papers required of me, and it cost me a lot of money. My father had to run from one state to another just to get my documents and send them to Curaçao. It took my parents more than a year before they could get all these documents together.

Some of these documents became invalid simply because my parents had to wait too long before the other necessary papers were received, and the affected papers had to be done all over again. Even the day I received all the documents in Curaçao, I was told that some documents were no longer valid, and my father had to start all over again. This was very stressful. I spent so much money, and my father and my brother suffered so much because they were running around for all these documents.

My father went back to the government offices to do all the papers over again, and I had to pay for them again. In Nigeria, before you can get your papers done, you must overcome many obstacles. The people working inside the government offices in Nigeria are so corrupt. After you have paid the government to process your papers, then you need to pay the workers again, or they will never process your papers.

When I received my documents the second time, all the papers were okay, the Dutch office in Curaçao accepted them, and we got married.

It had been fourteen years since I left Africa for Curaçao, and I hadn't visited Nigeria since then.

The entire family wanted to see me in person because it had been so long since I left Nigeria. My mother was worried and wanted to see me. My little sisters and brothers were all worried and wanted to see me. They had all grown up. Everything around me had moved so fast. I didn't realize that fourteen years had passed without me visiting my parents.

In February 2010, I traveled to Nigeria to visit my parents and the rest of my family. Unfortunately, I traveled to Nigeria when the country was in a terrible condition. I visited Nigeria without informing my parents that I was coming.

When I got there, the whole place looked totally different. I had to stay at the airport to call one of my kid sisters who lived in Lagos with her husband.

It surprised my sister to hear that I was calling her from Murtala Muhammed International Airport. She couldn't believe it. She was so happy and told me she was coming to pick me up, and so I waited for her at the airport.

My sister was thirteen years old when I left Africa. She had changed a lot and become a big lady. When she got to the airport, she was looking for me, and I was looking for her. I passed her without knowing that she was my sister, though I had the feeling that she might be my sister when I passed by her.

The face I used to remember had changed so much. It hurt me that I couldn't remember the face of my kid sister when I saw her at the airport. I feel so sad for some Africans who have spent most of their lives overseas without visiting Africa for one day.

When my sister finally recognized me, she was both thrilled and overwhelmed. She came to me and hugged me. She shouted, "Brother, brother," and she told me that my face had changed. I still remembered her face when she was thirteen years old when I left. I was happy that she was my sister, but she had changed a lot.

I felt so ashamed that my brothers and sisters had grown so big that they were almost like strangers to me. Everyone in my father's family changed a lot. I couldn't remember all of them, and they didn't know who I was because I had been away for such a long time.

My parents were so happy to welcome me to Aba, and they asked about my family in Curaçao. I told my parents that my family in Curaçao would come with me the next time I visited Africa.

CHAPTER 39

A New Nigeria Is Possible

WHEN I VISITED NIGERIA, THE entire nation was living in the shadow of many social vices and crime such as kidnapping and bank robberies. These crimes had grown unchecked to the extent that they were operating like businesses in some states of Nigeria. Even the police force in Abia State was afraid to face these gangsters and criminals who terrorized the entire city.

The month I visited Abia, there were many soldiers all over the city and on the streets, because the police force in Aba, Abia State, could not stop the kidnappings and robberies. The state government declared a state of emergency because there were too many kidnappings, and the federal government sent hundreds of soldiers to Abia. All of them were, however, corrupt.

They sent these soldiers to protect the cities so that the problem of kidnapping and robbery would stop, but they did not do their job. The soldiers were more interested in stopping the commuter buses and the taxi drivers to collect money from them. Any bus that was passing on the road had to pay 100 or 200 naira to these soldiers.

One day, I was on a bus going to the city, and the soldiers stopped our bus. They asked the bus driver to pay 200 naira, which was the equivalent of one and a half dollars at the time, before we could proceed on our journey.

I asked the soldier why they were collecting money from the bus drivers, and he told me they were not the ones who were destroying our cities with kidnappings and robberies. The military officer also told me that the money that they were collecting from the bus drivers was their salary—that the federal government sent them to Abia State without paying their salaries and would owe them for months. The terrible issue was that the government did not want to know how or what the soldiers did to get money to feed themselves. It had been rumored that oftentimes, the heads of government establishments would put the salaries of workers in their private fixed deposit accounts for three months or more to get an 18 percent or more interest up-front before finally withdrawing the principal money to pay workers in the fourth month.

Although the soldiers were everywhere in the city, kidnappings and robberies were still going on. I was afraid of being kidnapped because many people in that city knew that I had returned from overseas. People who return from overseas to Nigeria are often viewed as wealthy and successful and could become kidnap or robbery victims.

I spent only five days with my parents, and then went back to Lagos to stay for more than a month. I was communicating with my parents by telephone only while I was in Lagos. It was tough that after spending over fourteen years overseas without seeing my parents, I would return to enjoy time with them but be unable to do so. My mother cried because I spent only five days with them, yet I had to go to Lagos to stay because of the kidnappings that were going on in Abia State.

Gangs armed with heavy guns and ammunition were kidnapping people from the streets. My father had told me that I needed to be very careful while walking on the streets. It surprised me that the soldiers were there, and yet these gangs were kidnapping people and demanding ransom money from them. This was the reason I ran to Lagos, and I stayed there until the day I went back to Curaçao. My mother was not happy that she could not hug me or say goodbye to me in person before I went back to Curaçao. Nigerian leaders must arise and save the country from impending implosion by reason of corruption, kidnappings, killings, and armed robbery.

These problems accumulated over the years because of corrupt leadership in Nigeria, and our government did not bother to address them when they started. Today, things have escalated, and there is now a breakdown of law and order everywhere. I blame both past and present governments of Nigeria for the problems that we are seeing today, but a new Nigeria is possible. Yes, a new Nigeria is possible and will be possible when our youths, the victims of lawless and corrupt leadership in government, rise up, reject inducements, and vote in the right quality of political office seekers.

CHAPTER 40

A Word to the Endangered Youth of the World

When I visited Aba on February 2010, Aba was in a serious predicament. It had been abandoned by the federal government, and its residents cried out for rescue from deadly roads, flooding, and infrastructure problems. A lot of uncollected trash and garbage generated by the city population was causing massive traffic holdups, blocking most city roads. Solid waste generated was being dumped along the streets and major roadways.

The garbage on the streets and on the roads completely blocked up the drainage channels during the rainy season. Stormwater runoff from all parts of the city had nowhere else to go than to simply flood the entire neighborhoods. It is quite an unfortunate situation that Aba was facing.

The government and community leadership lack the will and capacity to do the heavy lifting required by the people of Nigeria. I was even told that our governors and local leaders had a special group that was into kidnapping and killing for their own political interests.

Truly, it is not unemployment that is the primary problem of Nigerians today. The problem is the greed of our leaders, and this has been with us for a very long time.

Kidnapping and robbery have become lucrative and common businesses for both criminals and our politicians. Many of our politicians in Nigeria are the ones who started these kidnappings and armed robberies. The political thugs they recruit and arm to do their dirty jobs while they are campaigning for political office are often abandoned without jobs after they get into office. Armed with guns procured for them by these politicians, and a boldness acquired from doing dirty business for the newly elected dishonorable "Honorables and Excellencies," they continue in the trade for which they already have the predisposition and equipment for—crime.

Nigeria is often referred to as the Giant of Africa, though it is still unable to produce a good leader, one who can lead this lovely country from the "Egypt" of massive corruption to the promised land. Like I said before, it's not just our government that has to be blamed for all the problems that we're facing today. We, the citizens of Nigeria, also have our share of the blame for encouraging our terrible leaders and our politicians.

Nigerian citizens have refused to expose and stand up to these corrupt leaders and politicians who live among us and throw their ill-gotten money around with impunity. We need to stop encouraging corrupt leadership by refraining from singing praises to them and giving unwarranted honorary titles to them.

When will Nigeria become like America, Europe, and the rest of the world? Many Africans have had to seek their fortunes abroad unnecessarily. If our government and the leadership of Nigeria had been living up to its responsibilities, I would not have left my country to go through untold horrors and the risk of untimely and painful death, in the bid to make a better future for myself and my loved ones.

Nigeria is one of the key destinations for global investment given her abundant petroleum, gas, solid minerals, and other natural resources. However, decades after our independence, Nigeria is yet to attain a tiny fraction of its potential. Rather, the nation has been under the burden of massive youth unemployment, and lack of basic physical and social infrastructure. There is no safe drinking water, no good roads, and no electricity. Tens of millions of Nigerians are presently living without electricity.

Our general and local hospitals in many states are in a terrible shape, and because the healthcare system is broken down, our leaders who are responsible for the state of things are going on medical trips and vacations to Europe, the Middle East, and America.

There is in recent times the rising incidences of terrorism and violent conflicts between cattle herdsmen and local communities, and this is threatening the peace and unity of the entire nation. There is indeed significant work to be done to turn things around, such as improving and supporting democratic development, rebuilding relationships between its citizens, and focusing on getting governance right.

Honestly, the Nigerian government has a lot of challenges ahead, and needs to be purged of corruption, in addition to prosecuting those found to be corrupt. Such a bold move would require a revolution, a complete turnaround of things. We, Nigerians, need to help ourselves and move our country forward, rather than sitting down and hoping that God will do the work alone. When we are called on to choose our leaders, we must make necessary sacrifices, reject their financial inducements to vote them into office again, and choose leaders based on integrity, capacity, and a proven track record. What we need in Nigeria is good and honest leaders whose true intention would be to solve all the problems created by the observed careless and wicked attitudes of our politicians.

I plead with world leaders and those international organizations that support the development of Third World countries, to help nations that are challenged by corrupt leadership by not allowing them to store their loot securely in their nations. When citizens and financial institutions of advanced countries are defrauded by Nigerian scammers, they request with evidence that such individuals be extradited to face legal action overseas. The government of Nigeria grants these requests. So, when things change in Nigeria, and a new and transparent government requests that looted funds be repatriated completely, we expect our partnership to be honored with the goodwill of such nations that champion democracy and fight corruption and financial crime.

The deleterious effects of bad governance and corruption in any nation have been quite evident in recent times. It has not affected Nigeria alone. Many countries in Africa and all over the world have their youth trying to get out because of the atmosphere of hopelessness created by bad and corrupt governance.

This situation puts most host nations in an extremely uncomfortable position, in which they are compelled to navigate through the decisions to either send them back or absorb them, and ultimately deal with associated public opinion that emanates from their actions. There are consequences for complicity, and there are consequences for indifference.

For the young person reading this book, who feels that his destiny is being choked to death, I have just a few words. The most important thing in life is to know God and to trust in him. It is possible that the frustration you are facing in those plans of yours is by the will of God. Nevertheless, if you trust in him, he will guide you, protect you, position you, prepare you, and settle you. Not everything that happens is ordained by God, but nothing can happen to a child of God without his permission.

Always believe in yourself, no matter any situation or challenge you may be facing—your hope for a better tomorrow is your legitimate right. Your ambitions, together with positive attitude, and prayers will have a profound impact on the final outcome of your quest. Keep on dreaming, keep on pushing, and never stop believing in God.

THE END

Acknowledgments

Special thanks to Abena Amponsah Anyaene:

You are my dream come true. I have loved you since the day I first met you and am blessed to have you in my life. I thank God every day that he heard my prayers and gave you to me as my wife. Words just cannot describe how happy I am to build a new life with you. Thank you for coming into my life. I know how blessed I am to be with someone as beautiful, intelligent, kind, and loving as you. I appreciate you and thank you for all the wonderful things you do. I'm so grateful to have you in my life.

Thanks to the retired Reverend Major Joe Twum, pastor at Royalhouse Chapel International (The Latter Rain Center), New York City, for all his encouragement, support, and prayers.

Thanks to Brigitte Josepha Assunta for her support throughout our journey in Curaçao.

Thanks to Mr. Charles Tay (Focus Photography) for helping with the cover design.

Thanks to Dr. Ike Odumodu for his input and sacrifice in the editing of this book.

Thanks to my senior brother (English Kess) Kess K. Anayo Chukwu Odili Chukwu, who teaches English and Portuguese language in Brazil, for his continuous advice and support.

I want to acknowledge Prestige Circle USA, a family-oriented social club based in the United States—"You are to me in this country, the family that I miss in Nigeria. Thank you for the togetherness you foster amongst brethren in the diaspora."

I would like to thank my family, to whom I owe a great deal. To my late father Humphrey Odili Chukwu Anyaene—"Thank you for the life you spent with us here on earth." To my brothers, "Thank you for your support."

Many thanks also to my sisters and my brothers-in-law.

Finally, the one person who has made this all possible has been my mother, Deaconess Joy Anyaene. She is a great inspiration to me; her support, encouragement, and prayers have made the entire family to draw close to God. A great deal of appreciation and enormous thanks are due to her, for without her understanding, prayers, and fear of God, I am sure I would not have lived to author this book and tell my story to the world. I thank you all.

www.ingramcontent.com/pod-product-compliance
Lightning Source LLC
Chambersburg PA
CBHW020928090426
42736CB00010B/1072